ADDICTION

IS NOT

A DISEASE

Marty Angelo

All Scripture quotations in this book are from the Holy Bible, King James Version unless otherwise noted.

Once Life Matters Ministries, Inc.
Website: www.oncelifematters.com
Website: www.martyangelo.com

ISBN: 0985107774
ISBN-13: 978-0985107772

MARTY ANGELO

CONTENTS

MARTY ANGELO

ACKNOWLEDGMENTS

Our Lord and Savior Jesus Christ
My parents "the late Dr. Martin and Marie Angelo"
My sister in two ways "the late Joanne Moeller" and her family
My brother Louis Angelo and his family
My daughter Brigitte and granddaughter Marie
My daughter Michelle and grandson August
The Lowe Family
Chaplain Ray Hoekstra
Charles W. Colson
Detective Frank Rossi
Judge Mary Lupo
Pastor Daniel Butler
Pastor David Wilkerson
Pastor Luis and Ana Lopez
Pastor Michael and Teresa Brown
Pastor Tommy Reid
Rev. Dean Webb
Rev. Frank Costantino
Rev. Garland 'Pappy' Eastham
Rev. Mickey and Laura Evans
Rev. Rico and Viki Lamberti

INTRODUCTION

This book is a combination of articles I've written since 2006.

The age-old argument of addiction being a disease versus a personal choice with real life changing consequences, will play on long after we are all dead and gone. I am only one voice in the wilderness trying to point lost and confused souls to the only real proven treatment that works; a personal relationship with our Creator... Jesus Christ. He is our Healer, Restorer and Teacher. Once Christ enters into a believer in Him, that person is never the same and becomes brand new, never again having to suffer from the ill effects of sinful addictions.

I wrote Chapter One back in 2009 entitled, "It's Called Sin: Doctor!" This article lays out my claim that what an addict is really dealing with is the ability to grasp the Truth of basic Christianity without all the extra added doctrines, dogmas and creeds that many of today's denominations have added to one's salvation.

Please read this book with an open mind asking God for whatever insights He would have you glean from it to either apply to your own life or to someone you are trying to help.

I have worked in prison and drug rehab ministry for over 35 years and have heard just about every excuse in the book why people are incarcerated or in substance abuse rehabs.

When I look back on my own life I can remember that I used almost all the same excuses for my rebellion and the self-inflected problems in my life.

It wasn't until I became a Christian in 1981 that I realized it was my unbelief in God and willful sinning that I was facing the rest of my life in prison.

I recently commented on Facebook regarding someone's habit that he refused to call sin. I explained that if he would acknowledge his addiction as sinful and repent... asking God to forgive him... that he would freely receive forgiveness and God would take away the desire to continue in his sin and cleanse him of the unrighteousness in his life (1 John 1:9). I also explained that the angels in heaven will rejoice upon his willful repentance (Luke 15:10). He continually refused and said over-and-over that he didn't believe his behavior was sinful. (Romans 3:23). I know for a fact that if he would have listened to my advice he would be free of his addiction today. I have witnessed it first in my own life and literally in thousands of others over the past 35 years of ministry.

The gospel is simple if only we would believe it and take God at His Word and allow Him to create in us a new heart.... becoming new creatures in Him with Christ living in us (2 Corinthians 5:17, Colossians 1:27). There is just no other way to be completely free of all of life's addictions (John 14:6).

It was my agnostic secular world's belief reasoning that I changed the word sin into addiction. The mantras for my 1960's generation was: "Turn on, tune in and drop out." I eliminated the word sin from my vocabulary and replaced it with: "If it feels good... do it... and the more I 'do it' the better I will be." However, just because I ignorantly thought I didn't believe in sin didn't mean God wasn't watching my every foolish move. When I finally reached my bottom and crossroads, He reminded me that He died and rose from the dead for my sins so I could be free (John 8:36).

01 IT'S CALLED SIN: DOCTOR!

Singer songwriter Michael Jackson's pre-mature death seems to be the hottest, saddest and most likely the longest story ever to unfold within the entertainment business. The entire world held its' breath while awaiting the popular singer's cause of death. Some in his family even called it a murder! One thing was certain; drug abuse was involved. On August 29, 2009 Jackson's death was officially ruled a homicide. (1)

As far back as 2006, members of Michael Jackson's family were terrified that his escalating dependence on prescription drugs had become a danger to his life – and even attempted an intervention in Las Vegas. (2)

When the media needs a comment when drug abuse hits the news it usually calls upon secular addictions medical specialists such as Dr. Drew Pinsky, the Piped Piper of celebrity substance abusers.

Jackson's death brings the subject of drug addiction front and center in the world media's eyes. In its quest to find answers, various media representatives such as Larry King only turn to medical professionals and attorneys with their questions.

Medical doctors identify and treat severe drug and alcohol abuse as a disease. (3)

While the media processed all of the medical and legal experts' jargon the Christian community seemed to have been forced to sit quietly on the sidelines with no one being asked for any input at all.

Doctors and lawyers were the only people being called upon in the media for opinions. Where were all the Christian ministers, pastors and teachers? Isn't what they have to say of any importance about Jackson's untimely death from a possible drug overdose?

I was asked to offer my opinion and insights during at a talk I gave at a California prison chapel service shortly after Jackson's untimely death. When I asked the inmate audience how many of them were in prison because of drug or alcohol abuse 99% of the 250 inmates raised their hands. They freely admitted they would not be in prison had it not been for their abuse of drugs or alcohol.

Not knowing the actual cause yet of Jackson's death at the time, I stated I was holding off in offering my take on the matter until the results of the autopsy were in. However, I did bring up the age-old debate on whether abusing drugs and alcohol is really a disease or a sin.

"When I researched the Bible while I was sitting in prison because of my drug use I found that type of behavior is sinful,"(4) I remarked and continued to share my insight: "Once I identified and confessed my behavior as sin I was able to receive forgiveness. I found that is the very simple solution to many if not all of my life's troubles, not just my substance abuse issues. And as an extra special bonus from God not only did He forgive my sins He took away the desire to ever drink or do drugs again. He also freely gave me everlasting peace, joy and righteousness."

'Drunkenness' is a term that refers to activities with definite spiritual and moral implications. Galatians 5:19-21 labels drunkenness as a sin, a real moral choice that will keep the offender from inheriting the Kingdom of God. However, an individual can be an addict or alcoholic without being a drunkard. The regular "social drinker," for instance, can still be a drunkard, without being caught up in the web of compulsive alcohol or drug use that characterizes addiction. (5)

"As drug abusers and drunkards, acknowledging our abuse as sin is our only hope for recovery," I informed the prison audience. "Once we identify and confess our addictions as sin we can repent and receive forgiveness. By receiving God's forgiveness will actually clear one's conscience, (6) which in turn, proves God is real, all powerful and loving. This is the basis of Christianity."

This may sound foreign, too religious or maybe even too simple to understand, however the Gospel of Jesus Christ actually still does change people from the inside out, transforming sinners into saints! Jesus Christ turns repentant sinners into brand new creatures in Him; not having to forever remain sinful powerless drug addicts or alcoholics." (7)

Barbara Brown Taylor in her book, "Speaking of Sin: The Lost Language of Salvation" states, "Sin is our only hope, because the recognition that something is wrong is the first step towards setting it right again."

Taylor continues, "There is no help for those who admit no need of help. There is no repair for those who insist nothing is broken, and there is no hope of transformation for a world whose inhabitants accept that it is sadly but irreversibly wrecked."

Taylor concludes, "Sin is our only hope, the fire alarm that wakes us up to the possibility of true repentance."

Substance abuse (sin) is only the tip of the iceberg in an addict's (sinner's) life. It is what is seen and felt by the substance abuser (sinner) and unfortunately the consequences are experienced and felt all too many times by friends, families and the innocent victims of the crimes addicts willfully commit.

The deep down root of the problem is sin and is what only God can touch, forgive and transform. It has nothing to do with treating sin as a "disease" as defined by the medical profession.

The Bible states that Jesus Christ gives believers in Him everlasting life (John 3:16). Along with that blessing comes the forgiveness of all past, present and future sins which is the direct result of receiving eternal life.

The Apostle Paul teaches: "Jesus Christ came into the world to save sinners" (1 Timothy 1:15). It is just as true right now… today in the 21st century as it was in first-century Christianity. And in the process of saving and forgiving sinners, Jesus takes away the cravings and desires to continue to willfully sin including any kind of substance abuse (sin).

What is missing in most doctor's attempt to correctly identify, diagnose and eventually treat addiction as a disease is an accurate medical test or exam.

A doctor can test an addict's blood or urine. However, the results will only show how much alcohol or the type, quantity or quality of drugs the patient has in his or her system.

Medical testing professionals do not and cannot actually identify drug addiction or drunkardness as a disease. There has never been an actual test developed that can do that. The lack of such a test clearly proves then that the willful abuse of drugs or alcohol is not a disease. (8)

"If… alcoholism and drug addiction cannot properly be identified as a disease with medical testing then what are they?" I asked the inmates in the chapel meeting. Many sat with questioned looks on their faces. I calmly, assuredly and simply stated, "They are called, sin!"

A doctor can test a so-called addict's brain. It is very easy to do that nowadays with modern technology, such as a CT scan or MRI. However, medical professionals must come up with an actual test that can *first* identify the person is an addict.

The addict's brain test may surely find some damage. However, the test results will only show the *effect* of the substance abuse but not find the actual cause *why* the addict used in the first place! Medical testing does not and cannot properly identify an actual substance abuse, drug addiction or alcoholism disease.

For example, the medical fields can expertly and precisely locate a patient's cancer or many other diseases through various reliable tests. However, there are not many people who are sent to prison or sit in a county jail cell because they have broken the law because they have cancer, diabetes or other easily identifiable diseases.

No one tries to use those types of diseases as excuses for wrongful behavior in a court of law. In fact, it can and should be very insulting to someone who actually does have an incurable disease to have self-inflicted drunkenness or drug abuse clumped in with theirs.

"Then why do drug addicts and drunkards try to use their so-called diseases as excuses when they get in front of a judge or jury in a court of law?" I queried the group of inmates and then went on to answer my own question.

"Because it starts with the medical field wrongly trying to identify sinful behaviors as diseases. This then allows a criminal to shun personal reasonability for breaking the law and instead uses the: 'I have a disease' excuse. They try to convince the court they are not responsible for their actions because they were either too drunk or too drugged when they committed the crime."

Most substance abusing criminals wrongly think they can get away with breaking the law because if they get caught they can blame their actions on their diseases.

If you want to really prove if drug abuse or drunkenness is a disease try attending a criminal's sentencing hearing. You will quickly learn first-hand that a prosecutor, judge and/or the jury do not believe for one minute that line of defense. The overflowing prison population proves it as well.

NO ... drug abuse and drunkenness are not diseases and the sooner a person comes to grips with that fact he or she and the rest of the world will be much better off.

A person does not have to remain an addict (sinner) the rest of one's life, especially if he or she follows the true teachings of Jesus Christ. He is here to set us free!

The first message of the gospel...

The first message of the gospel has always been to admit you are a sinner and be willing to "repent," meaning having godly sorrow for your sin and being willing to turn 180 degrees from it. Alcoholics Anonymous and Narcotics Anonymous and many other Anonymous type groups (there are now hundreds of them) have similar sounding teachings but they have replaced identifying yourself as a responsible sinner into identifying yourself as some poor irresponsible, powerless, sick and/or diseased addict. Right there is where one of the real problems lies.

Alcoholics Anonymous was originally founded on Christian principles.(9) However, their choice of descriptive words was changed so that the organization would not sound too overly religious. It figured people would not come to group meetings to seek help if they thought the groups had anything to do with organized religion.

A.A. officials wanted to only help people with their mainly self-indulged drinking problems and not for really offering to help change one's life permanently for the better through faith and trust in Jesus Christ. They wanted to leave that task up to the various churches.

The biggest problem with the AA/NA approach is that you are never officially healed but are tagged a diseased addict for the rest of your life.

Anonymous groups are somewhat effective. Their track record is about 3% recover. (10) However, that leaves a large percentage aimlessly hanging in the wind.

Christianity offers a whole new life! AA/NA principles forever keep oneself a powerless diseased addict. Many Christian treatment programs boast an upwards of an 86% recovery cure rate. (11)

If you abuse drugs and alcohol you first need to identify your own substance abuse or drunkenness as sin so you can truly repent of it. If you leave out calling any type of substance abuse as sin then you have nothing to repent of and receive forgiveness from. Therefore, you will still remain in a "sick" (sin) state for however long you care to call it that. You may never wind up believing or obeying the gospel. However, that is between you and God.

God is not going to force His forgiveness or deliverance on anyone. But, the fact still remains; Jesus Christ forgives sins today as He has for over two thousand years. This is the simple life-changing power of the gospel message.

There are millions of people over the ages who have overcame so-called and misidentified "substance abuse" and/or "drunkenness" as sin through the power of Jesus Christ without ever stepping one foot in an AA or NA meeting or rushing off to a doctor for a pill. The forgiving Gospel of Christ is not something new.

The medical profession is guilty of mistreating and/or misdiagnosing addicts (sinners) in trying to keep addicts in bondage to doctors, DSM-IV and ICD-10-CM codes, insurance companies and drug manufacturers. (12) It pays to keep one an addict! It pays big-time!! Just ask many of Michael Jackson's doctors. The money may be good. However, there are consequences even to doctors who fuel the fire of drug abuse to their patients. Dr. Conrad Murray, Jackson's personal physician is a perfect example. He was officially charged with involuntary manslaughter in Michael Jackson's death (13)

Doctors are not offering total deliverance from self-inflected addictions. Why? Most doctors do not have the slightest clue as to how to even begin a true and complete healing. There is also no DSM-IV or ICD-10-CM code for them to use so they can bill their

15

patients for their services.

"Many doctors do not even have deliverance and forgiveness themselves, which is why there are so many psychologists and psychiatrists who are just as confused as their patients." I stated to the prison inmates. "They are like the blind leading the blind."

The medical profession is only offering a temporary bandage for people's (sinners) substance abuse problems (sins) and one that has to stay on for the rest of an addict's (sinner's) life.

Doctors cannot offer their addicted patients any real life-changing overcoming power. They just continue to medicate, hospitalize and suggest secular counseling. In addition, addicts (sinners) are also ordered, many times by the criminal justice system, to attend the dreaded "never-ending" secular AA/NA type meetings for the rest of their lives.

Unfortunately, too many people have already moved way past any and all type of help by spending the rest of their lives either in prisons, psyche hospitals or worse; die from overdoses or suicide. Singer/songwriter Michael Jackson is the latest tragic example of such a life. Unfortunately, I am sure his death will not be the last entertainer to die from abusing drugs or alcohol.

Our Lord and Savior Jesus Christ came to set men and women (sinners) free. He did not come to earth to put people (sinners) in bondage to the medical profession. The Bible says, "They that are whole have no need of the physician, but they that are sick: I came not to call the righteous, but sinners to repentance. (Mark 2:17).

When the Bible clearly calls sin, sin (any kind… not just substance abuse)… then it is our responsibility to turn away (repent) from the, "if it feels good do it" mentality, and get on with a new life in Christ.

The Bible clearly teaches: "There is pleasure in sin for a season." Hebrews 11:25. However, it also says: "Your sin shall find you out." (Numbers 32:23). There are always consequences for sin in both Christians and non-Christians.

Sin, in any form, can NOT be covered or kept secret, no matter how hard we may try to conceal it. We might fool our wife, husband, family, preacher or our entire community, but remember: "The wheels of God's justice grind slowly, but they grind exceedingly fine." (Example - 2 Kings 9:35-37). We eventually do: "Reap what we sow." (Galatians 6:7-9). There are many examples in the Bible that prove consequences from sin do come. However, they come in God's timing not ours.

The Bible teaches God is an "if" God. If" we obey, He blesses. However, "If" we disobey He curses (Deuteronomy 28). He chastens/disciplines those that He loves. (Hebrews 12:6)

"It is fairly easy to see the direct consequences of sin as we sit here in prison." I remarked to the inmate crowd. Many shouted out "amen" in response. "This is not rocket science," I continued.

The entrance into God's new birth consists of believing the good news that Jesus is the Messiah who died and rose from the dead for our sins. Next is identifying ourselves as sinners (not as addicts), repenting (having Godly sorrow and the willingness to turn) of all known sin (including all substance abuse), confessing our sin to God and receiving the forgiveness and cleansing from the unrighteousness it brings.

We should then be water baptized in the name of Jesus Christ for the remission of our sin and then asking God to baptize us with His powerful Holy Spirit.

This process is very simple and was the first entrance statement as to how to enter the Kingdom of God stated by the Apostle Peter in Acts 2:38 on the Day of Pentecost in 30AD.

It is what brought people back in the 1st century and the generations that followed, and is what continues to bring us (sinners) now into the overcoming newness and power of life and right into the Kingdom of God.

Prisons will empty overnight if inmates would just receive, believe and obey this simple message. Budgets could be balanced. Rehabs would have to close due to lack of clients. Drug overdoses would cease. Bars and breweries would close. Judges, prosecutors and prison guards would have to find other lines of work. The reduction of victims of crimes would be so reduced that police forces would need to be decreased instead of having to always hire more officers.

The gospel is a simple life-saving message...

The Gospel of Jesus Christ is a very simple life-saving message. Yet many of today's churches seems to be forcing the secular world's media no other choice but to point out believers in Christ as a bunch of defected, delusional and/or miss-guided nutcases. It does not take too much effort to understand where that mentality comes from when you look and study many churches behavior and beliefs today.

The denominational Christian church is still so divided it is no wonder the secular media has a field day with it and only turns to worldly experts for advice. No one really seems to want or care to hear from Christians today about anything or anybody!

One of the main reasons many people could care less what Christians think about what is happening in the world is that a large majority of today's futuristic dispensational thinking church members live with their heads stuck in the clouds. They are waiting for Jesus Christ to come a second time in "this generation" to solve all of life's problems and show the world just how tough their God really is.

Many of this generation's futurist dispensational thinking churches preach and teach their special denomination will not be here for the return of Jesus Christ because they believe before He comes they will be taken (raptured) out of the world before the Great Tribulation begins. However, a very serious question to ask is: "Did the Great Tribulation already happen or is it going to happen in the future?"

Some futurists believe a rapture of the Christians will happen before, during, and/or after the "Great Tribulation". Therefore, these futuristic believers have developed an attitude that they do not care about what is happening in the world right now. As far as they are concerned the world is a lost cause and there is no need to "polish the brass on a sinking ship."

To make matters even worse; many futuristic dispensational thinking Christians today feel they do not have to go through *any* kind of tribulation at all yet alone the "Great Tribulation" in order to be a part of God's kingdom. However, the Apostle Paul teaches all Christians must go through much tribulation to enter the Kingdom of God (Acts 14:22).

The Apostle Paul certainly went through his fair share of tribulations (2 Corinthians 11:23-33). He did not pray to be raptured or taken out of the world. He gloried in his infirmities for Jesus (2 Corinthians 11:30). Is this what the churches teach today? Hardly!

Should we watch football or feed the hungry?

Many Christians cannot wait to get out of Sunday morning church services so they can get to the big football game of the week at the nearby stadium or play a round of golf. However, there is more to Christian living than just enjoying its' fruit. We are commanded to be doers of the word too by reaching out to the poor, sick, hungry, widows, orphans, prisoners, homeless, etc.

Who is suffering or going through tribulation for Jesus today? Too many Christians today think that this generation…(the one we are living in right now) is the one Jesus will return in. They are not even studying for themselves exactly what Jesus really taught. They want to change and twist Jesus Christ's words around to fit their own beliefs when Jesus clearly taught He was returning in the generation He and all the first century believers were living in (Matthew 24, Mark 13, and Luke 21). Not ours!

The correct teaching is Jesus Christ was already living within the first century Christians and did come *spiritually* in the clouds to bring judgment in the generation ending in 70 AD. The entire Old Testament religious system was destroyed and His everlasting spiritual Kingdom and overcoming power came in its' fullness at that time.

No one can live in the present, the now… if one's thoughts and behaviors remain in the past or are off somewhere in the future. There is no victory living in the past or placing false hope in the future. All we really have is today… the present…. the now!

Jesus Christ is a now God now. He is the "now" God of all yesterdays, todays, and tomorrows! Yesterday God was the "now" God then. Today He is the "now" God now. And tomorrow He will be the "now" God then.

The Bible clearly teaches that salvation is of the Jews (John 4:22). It all started with them. Christ came for the Jew first… then the Gentiles!

As believers, we need to make sure of when and where Christianity began. This is important because it affects how we are to live today… now! Christianity did not start as any one special denomination. Therefore, it is not based on who is in the right one.

God is not going to take one denomination of people out of the world (raptured) just to leave the rest of the other denominations to fend for themselves. No, all Christians are stuck with each other and the rest of the world, whether we like it or not. Therefore, we all have to contend with and live in the world now, helping to bring the life-changing Gospel of Jesus Christ to those people God brings across our paths. He does have a plan and purpose for everyone! The message is: "Love God first and our neighbors as ourselves." Everything else falls in place after heeding God's word.

The obvious people in serious need right now are drunkards and drug abusers. They are costing society trillions of dollars and causing countless numbers of pre-mature deaths.

Prisons are overflowing with criminals who committed hundreds of thousands of crimes because of their willful abuse of drugs and/or alcohol. Seven out of ten prisoners, in California, return to jail or prison within three years. This is one of the highest recidivism rates in the nation. (14)

The Second Jewish Temple was built in 20 B.C. by Herod the Great, though the surrounding outer courts were not completed until A.D. 64. The Temple was completed destroyed by Titus in the year A.D. 70, which Christ prophesied would happen.

God broke down the wall of partition between Jews and Gentiles back in the first century (Ephesians 2:14). That is the mystery of the Gospel; that Christ will live in both Jewish and Gentile believers, which is what was happening within the first century forward and what we have today! We are all one in Christ who have placed our faith and trust in Him.

God was never confined to a building (Isaiah 66:1, Acts 7:49). However, during the Old Testament days He did allow two temples to be built in His name. The temple was where the Jewish priests would go into each year to make animal sacrifices for "atonement" not forgiveness of sin. Forgiveness came later through Jesus Christ's dead, burial and resurrection.

In the New Testament, God forgives and spiritually enters into anyone who repents, believes and obeys the Gospel. Individual believers in Christ become the new spiritual Israel, the spiritual temple of God, the New Jerusalem, living in the spiritual Kingdom of God. Now! Today! Its is not about being a member of a *right* church or denomination… it is about individual believers being in Christ and Christ being in them!

One has to study what really happened over two thousand years ago to truly understand and appreciate what we have today; now!
There is no one select nationality, group or individual who is considered special in God's eyes. The Bible clearly states: "For all have sinned, and come short of the glory of God"(Romans 3:23). We all need forgiveness of our sins. That includes all races,

religions, nationalities, whether we are doctors, lawyers, preachers, teachers, celebrities, prisoners, drunkards, substance abusers. The list is endless. We are all sinners and fall short of the glory of God. All of us need salvation!

Jesus Christ came to give us life and life more abundantly... NOW. TODAY! He came to forgive and deliver sinners from sins. NOW! TODAY! We do not have to wait for this to happen, someday. Jesus and His everlasting Kingdom are with us NOW... TODAY just as prophesy pointed to. (Psalm 145:13; Daniel 4:3; Daniel 7:14; 2 Peter 1:11).

There are not any more biblical prophecies to be fulfilled. Jesus fulfilled all of them just as He said He would.

Jesus stated: "For these be the days of vengeance, that all things which are written may be fulfilled" (Luke 21:22). He was very much alive and living within the first century believers beginning on the Day of Pentecost in 30 AD and He also used the Roman armies in 70 AD to bring an end to the Old Covenant He had with Israel.

Jesus Christ used the Romans to bring about vengeance upon a disobedient, unbelieving and rebellious generation who had turned their back on their Messiah. He destroyed the old Jewish religious temple system and by doing so completed His everlasting spiritual Kingdom plan of salvation... with Christ living IN His believers.

Jesus Christ is in charge of building His church. In Matthew 16:18 Jesus explained to the Apostle Peter after he made the statement that identified Jesus as the Messiah that: "I will build my church; and the gates of hell shall not prevail against it." Jesus is building the church. Not man! Believers are supposed to be spreading, living and obeying the Kingdom message, not waiting around for Jesus to come again... when He has already completed His plan of salvation for mankind.

The futuristic dispensational thinking Christians of today are causing more damage to the Kingdom of God then they can honestly and properly understand.

No one can live in the "now" today if we are too busy waiting for a future physical earthly kingdom to come. People who are doing that are only repeating and believing the words of numerous dooms-day authors and so-called end-time scholars who some Christians like to call prophets.

These are actually *false* prophets who take scriptures way out of content and try to apply Jesus' words to the generation we are living in today. They should be teaching Christ's prophetic words were for the generation Jesus was actually speaking to back in the first century... not ours! This is critical!!

Jesus Christ predicted false prophets coming in His generation and warned His followers not to believe them or follow after them. This same principle should apply today. There have been false prophets in just about every generation since Christ but the ones Jesus was referring to were the ones living in the first generation. Not ours.

If Jesus said He was returning in judgment in the 1st Century then who are we to question or change His words? This type of attitude has always been a problem. We as humans want to "change" or "question" God's words to comfortably fit our limited minds, instead of allowing God's word to change and transform us into who He wants us to be.

A prophet is considered false when his prophecies do not happen when they said they would. A perfect example is all of them since the first century who have said Jesus Christ is physically coming again a second time. And there are thousands of them. Jesus warned of false prophets coming within His generation and the apostles taught that as well. (Matthew 24:24)

It is no wonder the secular world laughs at today's Christians. The futurist dispensational thinking Christians have wrongly followed misunderstandings or outright lies for years, thinking Jesus Christ is physically coming again when He already did spiritually back in the first century beginning on the Day of Pentecost in 30AD, and closing out that generation when He came in judgment in 70AD... just as He promised and prophesized. The Old Testament first prophesized this would happen within the first century generation and so did Jesus Christ. It did happen... and we have to learn to accept it and not try to change it around to mean something different!

The 21st Century church has turned into a wishy-washy watered down version of what God intended. The first-century church had the overcoming power of the Holy Ghost. The modern day church has basically thrown in the towel and holds defeated secular sounding AA type rehabilitation meetings in their sanctuaries. It has taken on the world's understanding of life instead of applying the Holy Ghost overcoming life-changing power of God.

The futuristic dispensational thinking church of today has become a medical treatment center calling and treating sin as disease instead of helping people receive real true deliverance and forgiveness from their sins. Many teach it is ok to sin. That God will continually forgive sin no matter how many times one commits it.

Christians should be asking ourselves; why has this happened and do something to correct it. We should not be waiting around for Jesus Christ to physically come again when He is already with us... *in* us! He is not going to repeat His plan of salvation all over again. It is up to us to accept and act on God's plan now and not try to get God to accept our own plan.

Many churches have bought into the addiction disease modality instead of offering total and complete deliverance. (15) It is a sad day to see this.

Are we really living in the spiritual Kingdom of God now? Once this issue is resolved in our own lives, individual problems as well as the entire world's problems can easily be solved.

Footnotes

(1) Jackson's death officially ruled a homicide
http://today.msnbc.msn.com/id/32598793

(2) Jackson Family Attempted Vegas Intervention
http://www.people.com/people/package/article/0,,20287787_20287851,00.html

(3) Treating Addiction as a Disease: The Promise of Medication-Assisted Recovery
http://www.hhs.gov/asl/testify/2010/06/t20100623a.html

(4) Drug abuse is equal to sorcery. A sorcerer was a person that prepared or used magic potions. In the New Testament the word "sorcerer" is translated from the Greek word "Pharmakeus", which comes from the Greek word for drug "pharmakon". English words such as pharmacy and pharmacology (study of drugs) come from this same root. The Bible calls sorcery a "work of the flesh" (Galatians 5:20-21), and clearly condemns sorcerers, saying they share the same destiny as fornicators, murderers, idolaters, and whoever love lies and live a life of lies (Revelation 22:15).

(5) Christian Recovery
http://www.alcoholicsvictorious.org/faq.html#disease

(6) **Hebrews 9:14** – How much more shall the blood of Christ, who through the eternal Spirit offered himself without spot to God, purge your conscience from dead works to serve the living God?

(7) **II Corinthians 5:17** – Therefore if any man be in Christ, he is a new creature: old things are passed away; behold, all things are become new.

(8) "Seeking the Connections: Alcoholism and our Genes." - Nurnberger, Jr., John I., and Bierut, Laura Jean. Scientific American, Apr 2007, Vol. 296, Issue 4. Psychiatric geneticists John I. Nurnberger, Jr., and Laura Jean Bierut suggest that alcoholism does not have a single cause—including genetic—but

that genes do play an important role "by affecting processes in the body and brain that interact with one another and with an individual's life experiences to produce protection or susceptibility".

(9) AA's beginnings - The Twelve Steps of Alcoholics Anonymous are basically a reliable and orderly approach to recovery from alcoholism and other forms of addiction. While Bill Wilson, the original author of the Steps, may not have been a born again believer himself, both he and Dr. Bob Smith did have vital relationships with people who were sold-out Bible-believing Christians. One of the prominent individuals (for whom Bill Wilson had great respect) was Rev. Samuel Shoemaker, a well-known evangelist of the early twentieth century. Some of the people involved in the beginnings of AA had come to Christ through a New York City rescue mission founded by Shoemaker. Also, through a fellowship movement called the Oxford Groups, they were both in contact with a number of sincere Christians. In developing the AA program, they borrowed from many different sources, including Biblical Christianity. The 12 Steps evolved out of six steps originally developed in the Oxford Groups. Their six steps were definitely Christian, as was the first version of the 12 Steps that were intended by Bill W. to be a more expanded outline of the progressive actions that lead to a new and changed life. It was only later, after sharing his first draft of the 12 Steps with some of the other early AA's, that the more overtly "religious" statements were edited out. We should not judge AA with the same standards by which we might judge a group that claims to be a Christian organization. It was never meant to be a Christian group, although there were some people involved in the beginning who would have wanted it to be. We might note that, even today, AA (practiced properly) does encourage people to get spiritual instruction and fellowship from the Church and other organized religious bodies outside of itself.

(10) "Treatment Doesn't Work" - Like Alcoholics Anonymous, treatment professionals claim success in the face of contradicting evidence. AA groupers boast "Rarely have we seen a person fail who has thoroughly followed our path." The truth is people rarely

succeed when following the path of those in AA. As stated previously, 95% of the existing treatment centers in the United States adhere to the 12 Step philosophies. Not surprising, the success rate of treatment is no different from the success rate of AA: 3%. http://www.baldwinresearch.com/index.cfm

(11) Teen Challenge Proven Answer to the Drug Problem. http://teenchallengeusa.com/docs/NW_study.pdf

(11) Teen Challenge U.S.A. Statistics. http://okteenchallenge.com/statistics.html

(12) The term "alcoholism" is a widely used term first coined in 1849 by Magnus Huss, but in medicine the term was replaced by "alcohol abuse" and "alcohol dependence" in the 1980s DSM III. Similarly in 1979 an expert World Health Organization committee disfavored the use of "alcoholism" as a diagnostic entity, preferring the category of "alcohol dependence syndrome".

(13) "Michael Jackson's Doctor Appears in Court" http://www.ktla.com/news/landing/ktla-conrad-murray-court-trial,0,2164347.story

(14) Public Safety http://gov.ca.gov/index.php?/issue/sgp-backpage/sgp-prison-reform

(15) "Eight Recovery Principles" - Celebrate Recovery - No mention of the word "sin or repentance" http://celebraterecovery.com.au/8principles.php

----

02 OVERCOMING CIGARETTE ADDICTION

I was a heavy smoker most of my life. I tried everything except identifying my habit as sin. I finally understood that the only way I could get rid of this deadly habit was to admit it was sinful. I Repented and asked God to forgive me. I physically stomped on my last pack of cigarettes and He immediately took the desire and craving away. I haven't touched one in years nor can stand the whiff of smoke in the air. It sickens me.

I know many people refuse to call smoking a sin and maybe that's what is standing in their way to overcome their habit.

It like an alcoholic or drug addict not wanting to call their addiction sinful.

That's most people's problem nowadays ... sin is now considered a bad word and has been stricken from one's vocabulary but it lurks and looms over all of us convincing us we can get one over on God... like He's not there and busy tending to someone else.

Sin is our only hope, because the recognition that something is wrong is the first step toward setting it right.

If we confess our sins God is faithful and just to forgive them and cleanse us from our unrighteousness (1 John 1:9). The Angels in heaven rejoice when someone repents (Luke 15:10).

When I am asked by smokers who are Christians what they can do to beat their addictions I advise them to try reversing their current stubborn attitude and do something so very simple: Repent! What do they have to lose?

As Christians we are taught that Our bodies are the temples of the Holy Spirit and that we should not continue in sin least grace may abound. God forbid. All we have left is sin.

Repenting .... which is something much stronger than just saying the word... It is action...

When we die to self and lust of the flesh is what repentance is all about.

Smoking brings death... it is even written on each pack or it was back when I smoked.

So... I say ... Don't quit... Repent instead. Then you come face to face with your creator. Leave it up to Him to bring you through. It is not a challenge thing but holding God to His word and like I said before... angels rejoice when we repent. So He is a pretty happy camper when we repent ... that's His way of dealing with our self-inflicted wounds.

Trust is a big issue. What? You don't think He will come through for you? That He really won't take away the desire? Is that the issue?

If you follow His plan then guess what? He gets the credit not your patch or doctor or whoever. God gets all of the glory and guess who will give it to Him? YOU!!! Your deliverance becomes your testimony and your testimony is exactly how you overcome along with His blood.

I am not saying I haven't suffered consequences from my years of sinful smoking.

Twenty years later I developed COPD that doctors attributed directly to my smoking cigarettes. So, I am not saying I got away scot free. Heavens no!

We all reap what we sow. God is not mocked. However, He did forgive my sin when I repented and asked Him to ... and He took away all desires to smoke, which truly was a real miracle to me because I literally tried everything known to man at that time and nothing worked. Nothing! And that is exactly where God brought me... to Him! When all else fails, where do we usually go?

When we should go to God first we sometimes go to Him way too late. But it is never too late to repent and let Him heal us for at least as long as we continue to remain on this earth.

You will not get away without consequences. You already know that or you wouldn't be searching for healing.

Galatians 6:7-9 – "Be not deceived; God is not mocked: for whatsoever a man soweth, that shall he also reap. For he that soweth to his flesh shall of the flesh reap corruption; but he that soweth to the Spirit shall of the Spirit reap life everlasting. And let us not be weary in well doing: for in due season we shall reap, if we faint not."

----

03 SUBSTANCE ABUSE TREATMENT CONFUSION

Throughout my 35+ years of Christian ministry, I have been exposed to numerous methods used in treating thousands of substance abusers. It was only in recent years that the term, "faith-based" surfaced onto the stage. I was always concerned of its' exact definition. I wondered why it was not just called "Christian-based." Are we that afraid to attribute anything to Jesus Christ anymore?

Calling substance abuse treatment "faith-based" instead of "Christian-based" opened up a door that I feel helped usher in what nowadays is a common running thread that blends many secular sounding "buzz words" with what the Bible clearly refers to as sins and the need of individuals to repent of them.

John-the-Baptist spoke some of the very first words in Christianity when he shouted out in the wilderness; "Repent... for the Kingdom of God is at hand" (Matthew 3:2). By telling people to "repent" meant there was some willful action expected on their part in return. They were not just supposed to stand there and look at each other or run to their physicians for a prescription. Repentance commands action.

Maybe that's why calling "faith-based" treatment instead of "Christian-based" sounds more acceptable. Christianity doesn't hide the fact that Jesus Christ and the Bible are the final authority on everything. Using the term, Faith-based leaves room for misunderstanding what or who the final authority really is. Some people may think that it's based on the words of the Bible but then again, maybe it isn't. Maybe it's a "blend" of the Bible along with the secular, medical approach.

The Bible teaches "sin" is the cause of most (if not all) of man's problems such as; disease, disorders, chemical imbalance, addiction, repressed memories, phobia, low self-esteem or a painful past.

Somewhere along the line in this current generation, the word "sin" has slowly been replaced with more easy to accept "secular" words such as "sickness and/ or addiction." It seems the words were added for the purpose of not offending or not scaring people from seeking treatment for their substance abuse issues. Unfortunately, if you really think about it; the omission of the word repentance has left a person powerless, which leaves them forever having to rely on doctors and/ or programs, and they are never completely set free.

Here are some examples of how this twisting of words plays out.

The Bible calls a person a "fornicator" who has sexual intercourse outside of marriage. It reveals in 1 Corinthians 6:18 that: "Fornication is a sin against oneself." The secular treatment community turns this around and instead of calling someone a "fornicator" the person is called a "sex addict" or "nymphomaniac" therefore, removing the personal responsibility of repenting (turning away from) of the sin off of the individual and making it sound acceptable.

The Bible calls a man a "thief" when he steals something or robs someone. Secularism turns this around and says the man has a disease and labels him a "kleptomaniac."

The Bible calls a man a "drunkard" when he drinks too much. Secularism also turns this around and states that the man is "sick" with the disease of alcoholism.

The Bible calls an out of control child who refuses to obey his parents or the law as being a "rebellious" child. Secularism diagnoses the child with a disease called "Oppositional Defiant Disorder (ODD)."

The Bible teaches that if a father doesn't provide for his family it's a sin. If a wife doesn't keep her house in order, it's a sin. If the children don't obey their parents, it's called sin. Secularism turns all this around and identifies these issues as the family having a Dysfunctional Social Anxiety Disorder (DSAD).

The Bible teaches that if a man tells one lie he is a "liar". Secularism teaches that the man has a disease and labels him a "compulsive" liar, making it sound like the man isn't responsible for the lies that he tells, instead, it comes to him as an uncontrollable compulsion.

The Bible says that overeating is a sin called "gluttony." Secularism takes the responsibility off the individual who overeats and states the person has an "eating disorder."

The Bible calls idolatry a sin and the person an "idolater" when whatever he esteems, loves, fears, serves, delights in and depends upon something or someone more than God. Some examples of different ways idolatry happens are: Pride makes a god of self. Covetousness makes a god of money. Sensuality makes a god out of the body.

Idolatry best illustrates both the in-control and out- of-control experience of addiction. It is outside the boundaries of God when turning to idols. The idol is a means to an end.

It isn't the goal of modern idolaters to be ruled by alcohol, drugs, love, people, food, sports, music, sex gambling or work. The goal of the idolater is to get what he wants. His desire is for the substance or activity to give him good feelings, a sense of power, to help him forget his troubles or his past. Whatever the heart craves is satisfied by the idol. Consequently, idolatry is and always has been rooted in the heart.

The secular treatment community has turned from even acknowledging the word idolatry and came up with a much easier and more comprehensible term: Obsessive Compulsive Disorder (OCD).

God cannot show mercy or apply pardoning grace if man does not consider himself to be a sinner and understand his need to repent (meaning having Godly sorrow for his sin and be willing to turn 180 degrees away from it). Sin and grace cannot be understood or measured without each other.

In Christianity, a language of grace requires a vocabulary of sin. Unlike disease, sin is something we can avoid and overcome. The Bible even goes so far as to state that God chastens people for their sins.

What the secular treatment community has come up with and blended into "faith-based" treatment are several Anonymous type groups that teach man is "powerless" over whatever problem he has. The responsibility is taken off the need for a man to identify his behavior as sin and his need to repent of it. The group replaces the word "sin" with "sickness" that a man has no control or power over.

Here are just some of the names of the many anonymous groups available today: Alcoholics Anonymous, Gamblers Anonymous, Emotional Anonymous, Overeaters Anonymous, Debtors Anonymous, Depressive Anonymous, Narcotics Anonymous, Smokers Anonymous, Women Who Love Too Much Anonymous, Sex Anonymous, Shoppers Anonymous, Liars Anonymous and many others.

Darkness is our only hope of knowing Light. Sin is our only hope of knowing life-giving grace.

Here is only a short list of real sicknesses that can be diagnosed using real medical testing procedures: AIDS, Cancer, Heart Diseases, Alzheimer's Cystic Fibrosis, Multiple Sclerosis, etc. It is insulting to those who suffer from such diseases to try to categorize drunkardness and drug abuse as a sickness.

A person with cancer cannot physically stop his cancer. However a drunkard can stop. Just lock up a drunkard in jail or prison and see what happens. HE STOPS DRINKING! He may still suffer physical consequences because of his abusive drinking that can trigger real diseases such as liver disorders, etc. but his drinking has stopped. There are no known tests yet developed to identify a disease of drunkardness, a.k.a. alcoholism/ drug addiction.

Sin produces some of the following consequences that affect the way we think and feel: Shame, personal guilt, depression, anxiety, fears, judgment, responsibility, sorrow and woes. Sin is more serious than, "I made a mistake, a poor choice; I'm sick" or placing blame on others.

There can be no grace where there is no guilt. No mercy for any sin. Sin in us is a part of our very nature. Personal sin is the root of most of our day-to- day problems. Sinful habits are the source of many of people's problems.

The secular model is sickness, rehabilitation and/or recovery; while God's model is sin, repentance and salvation.

When God created man He gave him certain desires and needs that, when kept in an appropriate context, would give him pleasure and joy. However, it is the world's goal to exploit natural wants and desires so that the physical desires rule. The world reverses God's order. Instead of people controlling their desires, their desires become idols that control them. They become enslaved, habituated and cannot say no.

When a "faith based" program attempts to treat substance abusers as anything other than sinners then the life-changing power of the Gospel gets watered- down into something that man comprehends as normal carnal reasoning instead of allowing the person, the sinner to be transformed by experiencing new birth.

A substance abuser doesn't need to be rehabilitated, which only brings that person back to where he/she first started abusing substances. It's actually self- defeating because substance abuse is only the tip of the iceberg of what manifests itself to the more deep- rooted issues or problems.

In a Christian-based residential program one can walk in as a drug addict and walk out a forgiven, transformed saint. The man or woman becomes a completely new person who is not "rehabilitated" but "regenerated." He or she is not sick forever but born-again by the transforming power of Jesus Christ.

This is something only God can do. Man has not the slightest idea where to even begin. Sure, many secular programs have some minor success, but mainly because they have "borrowed" Biblical principles and have instructed people to identify God as anything or anyone they choose. This is what most 12-Step programs are based on.

However, Christian-based programs introduce people to the real living and loving Jesus Christ who has not only defeated sin by His crucifixion and death, but also defeated death by His resurrection. These are two of man's greatest concerns.

This is why faith-based programs need to rely solely on Jesus Christ and not co-mingle secular sounding methods of treatment. If the Bible calls something sin, such as drunkardness, then people need to face that head-on and obey the Bible and repent and seek forgiveness and cleansing from God.

The Bible states in 1 Samuel 15:22 that "Obedience is better than sacrifice." It's okay to take stock of our lives and maybe attend Anonymous type group meetings, talk to doctors and psychologists about our problems and sacrifice for what we believe in and what we think is right and just. Nevertheless, do not think that it ends there.

For the true test of a Christian-based regeneration program is to teach obedience to the One who gives us life, the One who gives us breath, to the One who wakes us in the morning and the One who puts us to sleep at night. We need to be obedient to the One who knows what the level of our commitment is, who knows how to make things right and how to correct the wrong.

We should not change the Bible into something that makes us feel comfortable, warm and fuzzy. The Bible should change us. It will read "the same yesterday, today and forever." Jesus Christ loves us so much that He died and rose from the dead for our sins so we can live life more abundantly… now! We don't have to wait to the future for this victory. He is present with us right now.

There is no compromising once sin is identified. It can and should be repented of, asked, received and forgiven by God who then cleans us of the unrighteousness that it brought into our life. The Bible clearly teaches that the angels in heaven rejoice when a sinner repents. God happily forgives a sinner who is willing to repent and turn from sin. He hates the sins we commit but loves us, the sinners.

This mystery cannot be found in making God into a doorknob or a tree or whatever else one is taught in Anonymous secular-type groups. That isn't how God works. It's all about Jesus Christ being Lord, Savior and King of our lives, who is ultimately the author and finisher of our faith. He changes us from the inside out, burning off our own sinful nature as gold is refined in fire.

Secular man miss-identifies the spiritual power of God. He looks at the physical aspects of trying to understand the spiritual aspects of God through natural carnal means. He tries to figure out God in his head instead of in his heart. He needs to get his head knowledge of God down into his heart (spirit).

God is a spirit and exists in the spiritual kingdom realm. He is not easily identifiable within in one's head. His saving message is not physical – it isn't about recovery, rehabilitation or treatment. It is and remains spiritual, deep down in man where only God can consume the old sinful self-nature and replace it with His gift of life and life more abundantly. The gifts He then bestows on those who believe are what most people search for all of their lives such as; love, joy, peace, patience, kindness, goodness, faithfulness, gentleness and self-control.

The un-regenerated man tries to find these Godly gifts in so many other ways. The sinful nature of man tries to find these qualities by chasing after all the wrongs things in all the wrong places. Only God can give us the real ones.

Sin is pleasurable... man knows all about pleasuring himself. One of the only things that man doesn't like after all the pleasure wears off is the consequence that comes afterwards.

Therefore, allowing oneself anywhere from ten-to- twelve months in a Christian residential program allows enough time necessary to learn and apply Godly principles, so they never even think about abusing substances again.

God takes away the desire to sin and replaces it with his grace, mercy and love. These cannot be found in a needle, bottle or a pill which only bring pleasure and relief for a very short period of time.

I don't know one person who wants to remain sick forever. God has a different plan and purpose, which is a completely new life in Him.

Drugs, booze and all other sins are what bring us to Jesus Christ for forgiveness, grace and cleansing. We no longer have to remain bound by sin, but free in the Spirit of God.

----

04 CALIFORNIA PRISONS DRUG PROGRAMS

Numerous attempts were made to help solve the State of California's prison recidivism problem. The possible solution fell on deaf ears of two   prominent governors. In 2007 a report was presented to then Gov. Schwarzenegger that the state wasted over one billion dollars on years of proven failed substance abuse treatment within the prison system.

Letter to California Governor Mr. Arnold Schwarzenegger

Marty Angelo Ministries
Oxnard CA 93035

May 4, 2006

RE: Your letter dated May 1, 2006.

The State Capital
Governor Arnold Schwarzenegger
Sacramento, CA 95814

Dear Governor Schwarzenegger,

Thank you for your letter dated May 1, 2006 in response to the book I wrote and sent you entitled, "Once Life Matters: A New Beginning." You stated you have not yet found the time to read it but I would like to ask you to take a few moments just to read Chapter 17 entitled "The B Side" found on pages 193-203.

It should only take you five minutes to read this chapter but it could turn out to be the best five minutes you've ever spent in helping thousands of inmates locked up in the State of California's prison system and saving the taxpayers of the great State of California millions of dollars each year. This chapter discusses my involvement in a drug treatment program in Palm Beach County Florida entitled the "Sheriff's Drug Farm."

I noticed in the news you recently flew to the National Football League's owner's meeting to pitch your idea of the Los Angeles area having two professional NFL football teams because you know it will be good for our state. I am asking you to spend a few minutes of your time now to help the people of our marvelous state decrease the rampant crime and recidivism rate.

The Palm Beach County Sheriff's Drug Farm program was established back in 1991. It is an adult "boot camp" that emphasizes a Christian-based drug and alcohol treatment curriculum along with a military type physical discipline element. The two work well together. So well, that the results of a Palm Beach County Sheriff's Office study revealed that 88% of the inmates who completed this program have stayed clean and sober and were never re-arrested. I am sure you can agree with me that those are phenomenal results!

I would like to personally meet with you and some of your Department of Corrections staff to view a short 10-minute video produced describing the Drug Farm. I also have a Power Point presentation we could take a look at. I feel this type of program can work here in California and am willing to donate my time and energy to convince you and your staff of that fact.

If what you see and hear makes sense to you, I would also like to escort you to Palm Beach County Florida to tour the Sheriff's Drug Farm personally and watch the action live. I know it will change your perspective on prison reform.

Please feel free to contact me to discuss setting up an appointment to come to Sacramento to meet with you.

I know the majority of voters in the State of California would feel very fortunate to have a governor on board for another four years who could reduce the high crime and recidivism rate by 88%. The money saved alone would be worth it.

God bless you, Governor Schwarzenegger. I know you will approach this life-changing idea with an open, curious and enthusiast mind.

Sincerely,

Marty Angelo

Letter to Mr. Jerry Brown, Governor of California

Marty Angelo Ministries
Frazier Park, CA 93225

June 26, 2013

The State Capital
Governor Jerry Brown
Sacramento, CA 95814

Dear Governor Brown,

Back in 2006 I reached out to then Governor Arnold Schwarzenegger. Please see the enclosed letter I wrote to him back then and have posted on my website here.

I helped start an in-jail program in south Florida that was very successful. Upwards of 88% of the inmates who went through the program never returned to jail or prison. A government report and video on the successful program is enclosed.

I am again reaching out to our governor ... this time to you, Gov. Brown and State Senator Darrell Steinberg. The Senator is right when he states... "solve the recidivism problem and we will solve our prison problems."

It is too bad Gov. Schwarzenegger never took the time out of his busy schedule of looking for a football team to look into my solution. I hope you, Gov. Brown is more interested.

It is unfortunate that Palm Beach County closed this program in 2010 because of budget cuts. However, maybe California would benefit from a program such as this.
God bless you, Governor Brown. I know you will approach this life-changing idea with an open, curious and enthusiast mind.

Letter to Mr. Jerry Brown, Governor of California

Marty Angelo Ministries, Inc.
Frazier Park, CA 93225

September 10, 2013

RE: Prison Overcrowding - Email reply from Constituent Affairs - Office of Governor Jerry Brown - August 6, 2013

Governor Jerry Brown
ATTN: Scheduling Office
State Capitol
Sacramento, California 95814

Dear Governor Brown,

Thank you for your office's Constituent Affairs email reply dated August 6, 2013 regarding my June 26th letter concerning my offer to help you solve our state's prison problems. I stated in my letter that I agreed with Senator Steinberg that one the best and only solutions to our current prison situation is to reduce the number of inmates returning to prison.

You can release the entire prison population today and that wouldn't change a thing. Because according to national recidivism statistics 75% (three-out-of-four)* of those inmates will be rearrested and go back to prison within three years. California's figures are even worse with upwards of 80% returning to prison within one year! Therefore just randomly releasing inmates or placing them elsewhere is only placing a Band-Aid on the problem. It is not the cure or the answer to the problem.

A large majority of the inmates you are court ordered to be released will be back. If they are released without being changed it is only a matter of time. Most will commit new crimes and return to our already overcrowded prisons and jails... making matters much worse.

The substance abuse residential treatment program I helped develop while working for the Drug Abuse Foundation of Palm Beach County back in 1991 was called the Palm Beach County Sheriff's Drug Farm. It successfully ran from 1991 to 2010 and tremendously reduced recidivism with upwards of 68-88% of the inmates who graduated never returned to a life of crime nor substance abuse.

I am not offering to run or sell the state a similar program nor am I looking for a job. What I would like to do is bring all of my material, videos, budgets, reports and possibly two former staff members and a retired supportive Florida state criminal circuit judge to your office and meet with you and your prison and budget staff to explain exactly how this program works and how it can benefit the State of California. I suggest you invite some members of congress.

If you are interested and would like to try to start a similar program in one of the state prisons to test if the program will work, I am willing to volunteer my time as a consultant to help you bring this to pass. It can start small in maybe only one prison unit or pod to see if it works. I am also willing to promote the program within the criminal justice system.

We started our program in two small trailers next to one of Palm Beach County's jails with only a handful of willing inmates. The program grew tremendously over the years serving thousands of inmates. When the program closed due to budget cuts in 2010 it was helping an average of 150 inmates a month.
This program can easily be adapted within a state prison setting. It is a "want to" program so inmates across the system would apply for it. It would work perfectly for inmates who are within 12-18 months of release.

Again, I am not looking for a job but only to help set up and promote this program so that the inmates locked up in our state prisons will find a better way to live so that they will never have to return to prison again. This will not only help the inmates and their families but in turn will help our entire state.

In response to my letter dated June 26th your staff's email asked me to either send or fax whatever paperwork I would like to present and to pick a time and place for us to meet and what role I am asking you to play.

I would like to personally bring this information to your office as soon as possible. I know you have a very busy schedule and our prison problem is not the only item taking up your time so I will leave it up to you and your staff to pick the best date and time for our meeting. I am retired and can meet with you anytime. I would need at least a two-week notice so the former staff members and retired judge can fly in from south Florida.

Please have your staff contact me and I will be ready on my end when your schedule warrants.

We can meet in your office in Sacramento to make this as easy as possible. The meeting should only take an hour but if you need more time we certainly would be open to meeting longer or return at a later date.

Thank you for your time addressing this matter and I hope to hear back from you soon.

Please keep up the great work.

Warmest regards

Marty Angelo

Cc Senator Darrell Steinberg and L.A. Times Reporter Paige St. John and various press contacts via email.

Letter to Mr. Jerry Brown, Governor of California

Marty Angelo Ministries, Inc.
Frazier Park, CA 93225

October 6, 2013

RE: Prison Overcrowding - Email reply from Constituent Affairs - Office of Governor Jerry Brown - August 6, 2013 – 2nd attempt – follow-up

Governor Jerry Brown
ATTN: Scheduling Office
State Capitol
Sacramento, California 95814

Dear Governor Brown,

I am still waiting to hear from your scheduling office to set up an appointment to meet with you regarding my offer to help you solve the California prison problem. I sent you a reply letter dated 9/10/2013 in response to your scheduling office's email to me dated August 6, 2013. So far I have not heard a word back from your scheduling office to set up our meeting.

The recent voters' poll has indicated that the California voters are all in favor of rehabilitation instead of building more prisons, etc. I feel the program I am asking you and your staff to look at will address this very issue. The program I helped start in Florida was a success with proven outcome statistics. It worked with in jail/prison while an inmate was serving his or her time.

Even if you release the inmates the courts are demanding you to, you will still have many thousands of inmates still left in the prison system who need help and who will eventually be released.... and in most cases will turn right around and be back to prison within a few short months.

PLEASE ... have your scheduling office contact me as soon as possible. I think if you start this program small to begin with will certainly draw the attention of the voters and press who will look favorably on your effort to help solve the recidivism problem... and in turn ... save thousands of lives and millions of taxpayers' dollars. It is a "win-win" situation all around... and you, governor... will come out of it a hero!

Thank you for your time.

Marty Angelo

Cc Senator Darrell Steinberg and L.A. Times Reporter Paige St. John and various press contacts via email.

----

05 FREE FROM SIN

Jesus Christ came to set us free from sin. We can make it through life now and into eternity with His power from within. The choice between doing what's right or wrong becomes easy; when He's living in us... and understand it! We can be honest or deceitful; clean or unclean but it all boils down to obedience. Obedience is a word that people shrink back from when all it means is to follow God's instructions and I haven't found any of God's instructions to be harmful to myself or those around me.

1 Samuel 15:22 - And Samuel said, Hath the LORD as great delight in burnt offerings and sacrifices, as in obeying the voice of the LORD? **Behold, to obey is better than sacrifice**, and to hearken than the fat of rams.

The wise words of King Solomon, son of King David portrays himself as great in wisdom, wealth and power, but ultimately as a king whose sin, including idolatry and turning away from God, led to the kingdom being torn apart during the reign of his son Rehoboam. He sums up his whole life after everything was all said and done in the Book of Ecclesiastes.

Ecclesiastes 12:13 - Let us hear the conclusion of the whole matter: **Fear God, and keep his commandments**: for this is the whole duty of man.

The Bible teaches us, "To obey is better than sacrifice." What an incredible truth this verse is for our day-to-day lives. It supports the verses of Ephesians 2:8-9 which tells us that our salvation is by faith and NOT of works. While God is concerned about what we do with our lives and the fruit that we can produce for the Kingdom from our efforts, He is first and foremost concerned with our obedience. You see, our obedience flows from a heart that is yielded to Him, a life that is surrendered to do HIS will and not ours.

The Old Covenant had a strict adherence to the law. People just could not live by it. But in the New Covenant, Jesus Christ gives us the power to live an obedient life because He lives in us. The Book of Hebrews quotes the Old Covenant where it states, the Lord would write His law on our hearts so we have the ability to live an overcomer's life.

Hebrews 8:10 - For this is the covenant that I will make with the house of Israel after those days, saith the Lord; **I will put my laws into their mind, and write them in their hearts**: and I will be to them a God, and they shall be to me a people:

The Old Covenant scriptures concerning obedience continue right into The New Covenant; God didn't stop instructing us on how to live! He's not trying to force us to do anything but He wants us to obey for our own good, and His commandments are very clear.

Matthew 5:27-28 - Ye have heard that it was said by them of old time, Thou shalt not commit adultery: But I say unto you, That whosoever looketh on a woman to lust after her hath committed adultery with her already in his heart.

Matthew 7:24-27 - Therefore whosoever heareth these sayings of mine, and doeth them, I will liken him unto a wise man, which built his house upon a rock: And the rain descended, and the floods came, and the winds blew, and beat upon that house; and it fell not: for it was founded upon a rock. And every one that heareth these sayings of mine, and doeth them not, shall be likened unto a foolish man, which built his house upon the sand: And the rain descended, and the floods came, and the winds blew, and beat upon that house; and it fell: and great was the fall of it.

Matthew 12:50 - For whosoever shall do the will of my Father which is in heaven, the same is my brother, and sister, and mother.

Matthew 28:19-20 - Go ye therefore, and teach all nations, baptizing them in the name of the Father, and of the Son, and of the Holy Ghost: Teaching them to observe all things whatsoever I have commanded you: and, lo, I am with you always, even unto the end of the world. Amen.

Luke6:46 - And why call ye me, Lord, Lord, and do not the things which I say?

Luke 11:28 - But he said, Yea rather, blessed are they that hear the word of God, and keep it.

John 8:31-32 - Then said Jesus to those Jews which believed on him, If ye continue in my word, then are ye my disciples indeed; And ye shall know the truth, and the truth shall make you free.

John 8:51 - Verily, verily, I say unto you, If a man keep my saying, he shall never see death.

John 10:27-28 - My sheep hear my voice, and I know them, and they follow me: And I give unto them eternal life; and they shall never perish, neither shall any man pluck them out of my hand.

John 10:3 - To him the porter openeth; and the sheep hear his voice: and he calleth his own sheep by name, and leadeth them out.

John 12:25-26 - He that loveth his life shall lose it; and he that hateth his life in this world shall keep it unto life eternal. If any man serve me, let him follow me; and where I am, there shall also my servant be: if any man serve me, him will my Father honour.
John14:15 - If ye love me, keep my commandments.

John 14:20-21 - At that day ye shall know that I am in my Father, and ye in me, and I in you. He that hath my commandments, and keepeth them, he it is that loveth me: and he that loveth me shall be loved of my Father, and I will love him, and will manifest myself to him.

John 14:23-24 - Jesus answered and said unto him, If a man love me, he will keep my words: and my Father will love him, and we will come unto him, and make our abode with him. He that loveth me not keepeth not my sayings: and the word which ye hear is not mine, but the Father's which sent me.

John 15 - I am the true vine, and my Father is the husbandman. Every branch in me that beareth not fruit he taketh away: and every branch that beareth fruit, he purgeth it, that it may bring forth more fruit. Now ye are clean through the word which I have spoken unto you. Abide in me, and I in you. As the branch cannot bear fruit of itself, except it abide in the vine; no more can ye, except ye abide in me. I am the vine, ye are the branches: He that abideth in me, and I in him, the same bringeth forth much fruit: for without me ye can do nothing. If a man abide not in me, he is cast forth as a branch, and is withered; and men gather them, and cast them into the fire, and they are burned. If ye abide in me, and my words abide in you, ye shall ask what ye will, and it shall be done unto you. Herein is my Father glorified, that ye bear much fruit; so shall ye be my disciples. As the Father hath loved me, so have I loved you: continue ye in my love. If ye keep my commandments, ye shall abide in my love; even as I have kept my Father's commandments, and abide in his love. These things have I spoken unto you, that my joy might remain in you, and that your joy might be full. This is my commandment, That ye love one another, as I have loved you. Greater love hath no man than this, that a man lay down his life for his friends. Ye are my friends, if ye do whatsoever I command you. Henceforth I call you not servants; for the servant knoweth not what his lord doeth: but I have called you friends; for all things that I have heard of my Father I have made known unto you. Ye have not chosen me, but I have chosen you, and ordained you, that ye should go and bring forth fruit, and that your fruit should remain: that whatsoever ye shall ask of the Father in my name, he may give it you. These things I command you, that ye love one another. If the world hate you, ye know that it hated me before it hated you. If ye were of the world, the world would love his own: but because ye are not of the world, but I have chosen you out of the world, therefore the world hateth you. Remember the word that I said unto you, The servant is not greater than his lord. If they have persecuted me, they will also persecute you; if they have kept my saying, they will keep yours also. But all these things will they do unto you for my name's sake, because they know not him that sent me. If I had not come and spoken unto them, they had not had sin: but now they have no cloak for their sin. He that hateth me hateth my Father also. If I had not done among them the works which none other man did, they had not had sin: but now have they both seen and hated both me and my Father. But this cometh to pass, that the word might be fulfilled that is written in their law, They hated me without a cause. But when the Comforter is come, whom I will send unto you from the Father, even the Spirit of truth, which proceedeth from the Father, he shall testify of me: And ye also shall bear witness, because ye have been with me from the beginning.

Ephesians 2:10 - For we are his workmanship, created in Christ Jesus unto good works, which God hath before ordained that we should walk in them.

James 1:22-27 - But be ye doers of the word, and not hearers only, deceiving your own selves. For if any be a hearer of the word, and not a doer, he is like unto a man beholding his natural face in a glass: For he beholdeth himself, and goeth his way, and straightway forgetteth what manner of man he was. But whoso looketh into the perfect law of liberty, and continueth therein, he being not a forgetful hearer, but a doer of the work, this man shall be blessed in his deed. If any man among you seem to be religious, and bridleth not his tongue, but deceiveth his own heart, this man's religion is vain. Pure religion and undefiled before God and the Father is this, To visit the fatherless and widows in their affliction, and to keep himself unspotted from the world.

James 2:14-26 - What doth it profit, my brethren, though a man say he hath faith, and have not works? can faith save him? If a brother or sister be naked, and destitute of daily food, And one of you say unto them, Depart in peace, be ye warmed and filled; notwithstanding ye give them not those things which are needful to the body; what doth it profit? Even so faith, if it hath not works, is dead, being alone. Yea, a man may say, Thou hast faith, and I have works: shew me thy faith without thy works, and I will shew thee my faith by my works. Thou believest that there is one God; thou doest well: the devils also believe, and tremble. But wilt thou know, O vain man, that faith without works is dead? Was not Abraham our father justified by works, when he had offered Isaac his son upon the altar? Seest thou how faith wrought with his works, and by works was faith made perfect? And the scripture was fulfilled which saith, Abraham believed God, and it was imputed unto him for righteousness: and he was called the Friend of God. Ye see then how that by works a man is justified, and not by faith only. Likewise also was not Rahab the harlot justified by works, when she had received the messengers, and had sent them out another way? For as the body without the spirit is dead, so faith without works is dead also.

1 John 1:5-10 - This then is the message which we have heard of him, and declare unto you, that God is light, and in him is no darkness at all. If we say that we have fellowship with him, and walk in darkness, we lie, and do not the truth: But if we walk in the light, as he is in the light, we have fellowship one with another, and the blood of Jesus Christ his Son cleanseth us from all sin. If we say that we have no sin, we deceive ourselves, and the truth is not in us. If we confess our sins, he is faithful and just to forgive us our sins, and to cleanse us from all unrighteousness. If we say that we have not sinned, we make him a liar, and his word is not in us.

1 John 2:3-6 - And hereby we do know that we know him, if we keep his commandments. He that saith, I know him, and keepeth not his commandments, is a liar, and the truth is not in him. But whoso keepeth his word, in him verily is the love of God perfected: hereby know we that we are in him. He that saith he abideth in him ought himself also so to walk, even as he walked.

1 John 2:17 - And the world passeth away, and the lust thereof: but he that doeth the will of God abideth forever.

1 John 3:22-23 - And whatsoever we ask, we receive of him, because we keep his commandments, and do those things that are pleasing in his sight. And this is his commandment, That we should believe on the name of his Son Jesus Christ, and love one another, as he gave us commandment.

2 John 1:6 - And this is love, that we walk after his commandments. This is the commandment, That, as ye have heard from the beginning, ye should walk in it.

2 John 1:9 - Whosoever transgresseth, and abideth not in the doctrine of Christ, hath not God. He that abideth in the doctrine of Christ, he hath both the Father and the Son

Revelation 12:17 - And the dragon was wroth with the woman, and went to make war with the remnant of her seed, which keep the commandments of God, and have the testimony of Jesus Christ.

Revelation 22:14 - Blessed are they that do his commandments, that they may have right to the tree of life, and may enter in through the gates into the city.

By making correct choices blessings come along with them naturally. Under the old covenant, Deuteronomy 28 outlined the expected outcome to Gods people concerning their choices. The New Covenant's expected outcome can be found in Galatians under the laws of reaping and sowing. Either way our rewards or chastisement will manifest in direct line with our actions.

The difference between the Old and the New is that we have Christ in us! We have the Old Covenant believers at a strong disadvantage. We have the same power available to us that came into the Apostles on the Day of Pentecost; so it's hard to understand why so many believers are all bound up in sin, confusion and despair.

I think that when a person cries out to God for mercy, because they're in the midst of a devastating trial and He shows up; they get that first, thirst quenching drink of water that brings along with it a feeling of freedom and untainted love. Then a preacher or a sweet child of Christ comes along and tells them how rich in mercy and abounding in love He is.

"There is nothing that you could do, that God won't forgive you." They say, and there it stops.

God has so much more! People need to delve into the scriptures for themselves and learn His plan in its entirety. Many just skim right past the tough stuff *or* believe He's coming to save them soon.

Let me tell you how I know this: I see thousands of inmates go in-and-out of our nation's prisons and many of them profess to be Christians. Most have no clue of what went so wrong that they had to go back. Who left who? God didn't leave them. He promises to never leave us.

What happens is; they sit in a jail cell and pull promises out of the Bible as if they were playing the lottery. They want what God has to offer without doing what God says to get there! Those inmates know that God loves them, but ask them how many of them got a, "Get out of Jail Free Card." God doesn't want them, or any of us to get away with lawlessness, or going against what He says and we know is right.

The same thing is happening to many people in the church today but it's much more subtle because the problems and habits are a lot less physically dangerous. However, their problems are problems none the less. Strife, envy, gossip, mountains of debt, drunkardness, pornography and adultery (just to name a few) are running rampant in the lives of many of today's church members but none of it is illegal. That's the only difference between the incarcerated and the believers sitting in the pews but it all boils down to sin! God isn't rating it either. There's no scale from one-to-ten with Him.

I sometimes think that the people in prison are the fortunate ones. At least they know they are in a prison! Their chains are visible. Their trials and tribulations are devastating enough to shake some of them from their spiritual apathy (it worked for me). They get a great big slap, where many of the people in the church just get used to living with one-foot-in and one-foot-out, so they walk around powerless. They're stuck in the middle of being saved, and—being free indeed!

Obedience to God equals real freedom but not many see it that way. God loves us but He's a God that won't be mocked, we will reap whatever we sow, it's not the devil's fault—he is defeated in a believer's life! God knows how easily we can deceive ourselves, that's why He made it a point to tell us not to! Why not focus on this for a while? Church attendance may go down for a time but Holy Ghost power would be turned up!

Revelation 22:11 - He that is unjust, let him be unjust still: and he which is filthy, let him be filthy still: and he that is righteous, let him be righteous still: and he that is holy, let him be holy still.

Matthew 5:45 - That ye may be the children of your Father which is in heaven: for he maketh his sun to rise on the evil and on the good, and sendeth rain on the just and on the unjust.

Galatians5:18-25 - But if ye be led of the Spirit, ye are not under the law. Now the works of the flesh are manifest, which are these; Adultery, fornication, uncleanness, lasciviousness, Idolatry, witchcraft, hatred, variance, emulations, wrath, strife, seditions, heresies, Envyings, murders, drunkenness, revelings, and such like: of the which I tell you before, as I have also told you in time past, that **they which do such things shall not inherit the kingdom of God**. But the fruit of the Spirit is love, joy, peace, long suffering, gentleness, goodness, faith, Meekness, temperance: against such there is no law. And they that are Christ's have crucified the flesh with the affections and lusts. If we live in the Spirit, let us also walk in the Spirit.

Ephesians 5:2-4 - And walk in love, as Christ also hath loved us, and hath given himself for us an offering and a sacrifice to God for a sweetsmelling savour. But fornication, and all uncleanness, or covetousness, let it not be once named among you, as becometh saints; Neither filthiness, nor foolish talking, nor jesting, which are not convenient: but rather giving of thanks.

Colossians3:5 - Mortify therefore your members which are upon the earth; fornication, uncleanness, inordinate affection, evil concupiscence, and covetousness, which is idolatry:

1 Thessalonians 4:2-4 - For ye know what commandments we gave you by the Lord Jesus. For this is the will of God, even your sanctification, that ye should abstain from fornication: That every one of you should know how to possess his vessel in sanctification and honour;

1Peter3:18 - For Christ also hath once suffered for sins, the just for the unjust, that he might bring us to God, being put to death in the flesh, but quickened by the Spirit:

Galatians 6:7 - Be not deceived; God is not mocked: for whatsoever a man soweth, that shall he also reap.

When we give into sin, it's like throwing a huge rock into the calm waters of our soul. Everything becomes chaotic and bothersome. It often takes time for the waters to calm down and become peaceful again. The apostle Peter knew this when he said, "I beseech you as strangers and pilgrims, abstain from fleshly lusts, which war against the soul" (1 Peter 2:11).

----

06 VICTORY TODAY

Please do not put off until tomorrow the victory you can have today.

Satan was defeated over two thousand years ago and his works were destroyed at the crucifixion and resurrection of Jesus Christ and His spiritual coming as the Holy Ghost on the Day of Pentecost and in judgment in AD 70! Satan's grip on the world was destroyed through Christ.

There is no reason why Christians should acknowledge the devil has any control in their lives once we've placed our faith and trust in Jesus.

Through Jesus Christ's shed blood and Holy Ghost overcoming power we can live righteously now through obedience, faith and power in God's Word.

1 John 3:8 - He that committeth sin is of the devil; for the devil sinneth from the beginning. For this purpose the Son of God was manifested, that he might destroy the works of the devil.

The King came, He comes

As today's Church we need to realize that we have the authority over evil. We are not to be led around thinking that we are just "poor powerless Christians" with no ability to overcome.

We should not and need not wait for Jesus to "come again" but next time as King. He already did come and fulfilled the old Jewish covenant, which by doing so allowed open access to His Kingdom once and for all. He continues to come to anyone who receives Him into his or her heart. The victory is ours by believing and receiving.

John 18:37 - Pilate therefore said unto him, Art thou a king then? **Jesus answered, Thou sayest that I am a king. To this end was I born, and for this cause came I into the world**, that I should bear witness unto the truth. Every one that is of the truth heareth my voice.

John 10:10 - The thief cometh not, but for to steal, and to kill, and to destroy: I am come that they might have life, and that they might have it more abundantly.

Overcoming Power

There are many examples in the Bible of people who faced difficulties as believers and overcame. We can model our lives after them and even face physical death knowing that even the sting has been removed.

Revelation 12:11 - And **they overcame** him by the blood of the Lamb, and by the word of their testimony; and they loved not their lives unto the death.

1 John 4:4 - Ye are of God, little children, and **have** overcome them: because greater is he that is in you, than he that is in the world.

John 16:33 - These things I have spoken unto you, that in me ye might have peace. In the world ye shall have tribulation: but be of good cheer; **I have overcome the world.**

1 Corinthians 15:55 - O death, where is thy sting? O grave, where is thy victory?

Death and Resurrection

Martha misunderstood the idea of death and resurrection when she told Jesus that she knew that Lazarus would rise from the dead at the last day.

John 11:24 - Martha saith unto him, I know that he shall rise again in the resurrection at the last day.

Jesus explained to Martha that He is the resurrection and it had nothing to do with being physically raised from the dead.

John 11:25-26 - Jesus said unto her, **I am the resurrection**, and the life: he that **believeth in me,** though he were dead, yet shall he live: **And whosoever liveth and believeth in me shall never die**. Believest thou this?

There is no reason to wait for a physical resurrection to live a resurrected life. The Jews waited for a physical resurrection to happen and it did in AD 70 (the last day… the time of the end). However, we as Christians can live a resurrected life right now, today by believing in Jesus who is the resurrection.

2 Timothy 2:11 - It is a faithful saying: For if we be dead with him, we shall also live with him:

Colossians 2:12 - Buried with him in baptism, wherein also **ye are risen with him** through the faith of the operation of God, who hath raised him from the dead.

Colossians 3:1-3 - **If ye then be risen with Christ,** seek those things which are above, where Christ sitteth on the right hand of God. Set your affection on things above, not on things on the earth. For ye are dead, and your life is hid with Christ in God.

Colossians 3 gives us a glimpse of what a believer's life means in light of Christ's resurrection. It says that you, as a believer, have already been brought into resurrection union with Jesus Christ. For this reason, we must correct a common misunderstanding.

Usually when believers think of their resurrection, they think that it's an event which will take place exclusively in the future—at the time of Christ's second coming.

If this is how you understand your resurrection, then you do not fully understand the dynamic of Christ's resurrection.

For the Bible teaches that the believer's resurrection took place over two-thousand years ago… notice the past tense in verse 1: "If ye then ye be risen with Christ." Thus, Christ's resurrection is the active dynamic which resurrects all believers (past, present and future). Christ did not rise from the dead in isolation. Rather, the power of Christ's resurrection brought life to all of his people, those who have lived and those who will live.

Matthew 22:32 - I am the God of Abraham, and the God of Isaac, and the God of Jacob? **God is not the God of the dead, but of the living.**

We can follow Apostle Paul's teachings and die to our old nature and live according to God's Kingdom principles to the fullest, NOW!

Romans 6:8-11 - Now if we be dead with Christ, we believe that we shall also live with him: Knowing that Christ being raised from the dead dieth no more; death hath no more dominion over him. For in that he died, he died unto sin once: but in that he liveth, he liveth unto God. Likewise reckon ye also yourselves to be dead indeed unto sin, but alive unto God through Jesus Christ our Lord.

2 Corinthians 5:17 - **Therefore if any man be in Christ, he is a new creature:** old things are passed away; behold, all things are become new.

Romans 12:1-2 - I beseech you therefore, brethren, by the mercies of God, that ye present your bodies a living sacrifice, holy, acceptable unto God, which is your reasonable service. And be not conformed to this world: but be ye transformed by the renewing of your mind, that ye may prove what is that good, and acceptable, and perfect, will of God.

Obey God and Live

Jesus Christ came to give us life and life more abundantly and in return commands us to obey Him.

John 10:10 - The thief cometh not, but for to steal, and to kill, and to destroy: **I am come that they might have life,** and that they might have it more abundantly.

Luke 11:28 - But he said, Yea rather, blessed [are] they that hear the word of God, **and keep it.**

The Apostles paid the price

The Bible teaches that after the Day of Pentecost the twelve Apostles were willing to serve God no matter what price they had to pay! They knew that they would live forever, even though they had to lay down their physical lives.

2 Timothy 2:12 - If we suffer, we shall also reign with him: if we deny him, he also will deny us:

The Apostles' full power began when Christ as Holy Ghost came fully into their lives on the Day of Pentecost. Once that happened, they knew that there was more to God than what their Jewish religion and religious leaders of their day offered. Jesus opened their eyes to scripture before and after the resurrection but on the Day of Pentecost, He came spiritually in them as the Holy Ghost so they completely understood exactly who Jesus was and what laid ahead for them and future believers as well with judgment coming within their generation.

Luke 24:44-49 - And he said unto them, These are the words which I spake unto you, while I was yet with you, that all things must be fulfilled, which were written in the law of Moses, and in the prophets, and in the psalms, concerning me. **Then opened he**

their understanding, that they might understand the scriptures, And said unto them, Thus it is written, and thus it behooved Christ to suffer, and to rise from the dead the third day: And that repentance and remission of sins should be preached in his name among all nations, beginning at Jerusalem. And ye are witnesses of these things. And, behold, **I send the promise of my Father upon you: but tarry ye in the city of Jerusalem, until ye be endued with power from on high.**

<u>Acts 1:1-5</u> - The former treatise have I made, O Theophilus, of all that Jesus began both to do and teach, Until the day in which he was taken up, after that he through the Holy Ghost had given commandments unto the apostles whom he had chosen: To whom also he shewed himself alive after his passion by many infallible proofs, being seen of them forty days, and speaking of the things pertaining to the kingdom of God: And, being assembled together with them, **commanded them that they should not depart from Jerusalem, but wait for the promise of the Father, which, saith he, ye have heard of me. For John truly baptized with water; but ye shall be baptized with the Holy Ghost not many days hence.**

Abraham Looked for a City

Old Testament Abraham "looked for" and expected a "City"… "What city?" You may ask: "Is this city with us right now?"

<u>**Hebrews 11:10,16**</u> - For he looked for a city which hath foundations, whose builder and maker is God. - **11:6** - But **now** they desire a better country, that is, an heavenly1: wherefore God is not ashamed to be called their God: for he hath prepared for them a city.

----

07 THE KINGDOM OF GOD

God's promised kingdom has always been a spiritual one. It took faith to be a part of it, but not faith in the Jewish law but faith in the "SEED" (Jesus) who came through Abraham.

Galatians 3:16 - Now to Abraham and his seed were the promises made. He saith not, And to seeds, as of many; but as of one, And to thy seed, which is Christ.

Hebrews 11:13-16 - These all died in faith, not having received the promises, but having seen them afar off, and were persuaded of them, and embraced them, and confessed that they were strangers and pilgrims on the earth. For they that say such things declare plainly that they seek a country. And truly, if they had been mindful of that country from whence they came out, they might have had opportunity to have returned. But now they desire a better country, that is, an heavenly: wherefore God is not ashamed to be called their God: for he hath prepared for them a city.

God is a Spirit

John 4:24 - God is a Spirit: and they that worship him must worship him in spirit and in truth.

Yes, God did manifest Himself as man, Jesus, born of a virgin according to scripture. However, He was still God. Jesus was *made* both Lord and Christ, taking the Name of His everlasting Father.

John 14:20 - At that day (Pentecost) ye shall know that I [am] in my Father, and ye in me, and **I in you**.

Acts 2:36 - Therefore let all the house of Israel know assuredly, **that God hath made the same Jesus, whom ye have crucified, both Lord and Christ.**

John 14:9 - Jesus saith unto him, Have I been so long time with you, and yet hast thou not known me, Philip? **he that hath seen me hath seen the Father;** and how sayest thou [then], Shew us the Father?

Isaiah 9:6 - For unto us a child is born, unto us a son is given: and the government shall be upon his shoulder: and his name shall be called Wonderful, Counseller, The mighty God, **The everlasting Father, The Prince of Peace.**

God's spiritual church is made with His own Hands; which He promised He would never leave or forsake. He gives believers the power to overcome sin through repentance and forgiveness and the ability to live righteously each and every day because He mysteriously lives in them.

Colossians 1:26-28 - Even the mystery which hath been hid from ages and from generations, but now is made manifest to his saints: To whom God would make known what is the riches of the glory of this mystery among the Gentiles; which is **Christ in you,** the hope of glory: Whom we preach, warning every man, and teaching every man in all wisdom; that we may present every man perfect in Christ Jesus:

Hebrews 13:5 - Let your conversation be without covetousness; and be content with such things as ye have: for he hath said, I will never leave thee, nor forsake thee.

2 Corinthians 13:5 - Examine yourselves, whether ye be in the faith; prove your own selves. Know ye not your own selves, **how that Jesus Christ is in you**, except ye be reprobates?

Galatians 1:16 - **To reveal his Son in me**, that I might preach him among the heathen; immediately I conferred not with flesh and blood:

John 6:53-58 - Then Jesus said unto them, Verily, verily, I say unto you, Except ye eat the flesh of the Son of man, and drink his blood, ye have no life in you. Whoso eateth my flesh, and drinketh my blood, hath eternal life; and I will raise him up at the last day. For my flesh is meat indeed, and my blood is drink indeed. **He that eateth my flesh, and drinketh my blood, dwelleth in me, and I in him.** As the living Father hath sent me, and I live by the Father: so he that eateth me, even he shall live by me. This is that bread which came down from heaven: not as your fathers did eat manna, and are dead: **he that eateth of this bread shall live for ever.**

Galatians 2:20 - I am crucified with Christ: nevertheless I live; yet not I, but **Christ liveth in me**: and the life which I now live in the flesh I live by the faith of the Son of God, who loved me, and gave himself for me.

Galatians   4:6 - And because ye are sons, God hath sent forth the Spirit of his Son into your hearts, crying, Abba, Father.

Galatians 6:18 - Brethren, the grace of **our Lord Jesus Christ be with your spirit**. Amen.

Jesus Christ is the "Door"

John 10:9 - I am the door: by me if any man enter in, he shall be saved, and shall go in and out, and find pasture.

Jesus is not referring to an actual pasture in the above scripture, just as it does not mean believers are literal sheep. Jesus Christ is not an actual physical door either. He is Spirit and His New Jerusalem Kingdom is spiritual! This kingdom is not one we have to wait for. Jesus is the everlasting Kingdom of God with Him being King of all believers right now... whether they know and acknowledge it or not.

Whenever a person first believes in Jesus, whether Jew or Gentile, they become one spiritually with God and Christ enters into them. This kingdom is not a democracy or a republic where one is given the choice to negotiate on how to live in it.

A kingdom can only be ruled by one person, the King. This is one of the reasons why most Westerners don't have the slightest idea on what it's like to live in an actual kingdom where the king owns and rules everything.

The Old Testament Jews knew what it was like to live under an actual physical king, yet all the while God was spiritually the real King. However, during the first century and forward they (Jews and later Gentiles) had to drop the physical aspect of a king and come through Jesus, in order to have the Kingdom of God enter into them. Many didn't learn or want to experience the simple transition. They had the wrong concept of the Kingdom of God, just like many living in the generations following up to and including today's. There is no longer a kingdom for just Jews. Jesus is now the Door for both Jews and Gentiles. All have to come through the same Door, to have the Kingdom of God enter into them and become a part of their lives.

Mark 1:15 - And saying, **The time is fulfilled, and the kingdom of God is at hand:** repent ye, and believe the gospel.

Galatians 3:13-14 - Christ hath redeemed us from the curse of the law, being made a curse for us: for it is written, Cursed is every one that hangeth on a tree: **That the blessing of Abraham might come on the Gentiles through Jesus Christ; that we might receive the promise of the Spirit through faith.**

Galatians 3:28 - **There is neither Jew nor Greek,** there is neither bond nor free, there is neither male nor female: for ye are all one in Christ Jesus.

Romans 9:24-26 - Even us, whom he hath called, **not of the Jews only, but also of the Gentiles?** As he saith also in Osee, I will call them my people, which were not my people; and her beloved, which was not beloved. And it shall come to pass, that in the place where it was said unto them, Ye are not my people; there shall they be called the children of the living God.

Psalm 145:13 - Thy kingdom is an everlasting kingdom, and thy dominion endureth throughout all generations.

Daniel 4:3 - How great are his signs! and how mighty are his wonders! his kingdom is an everlasting kingdom, and his dominion is from generation to generation.

Daniel 7:27 - And the kingdom and dominion, and the greatness of the kingdom under the whole heaven, shall be given to the people of the saints of the most High, whose kingdom is an everlasting kingdom, and all dominions shall serve and obey him.

2 Peter 1:11 - For so an entrance shall be ministered unto you abundantly into the everlasting kingdom of our Lord and Saviour Jesus Christ.

If an American or anyone else living in a democratic society doesn't like a presidential or congressional candidate who is running for office, he or she has the choice to vote for and support a different candidate. Not so in the Kingdom of God. There are no other candidates.

The Kingdom of God is officially ruled by Jesus Christ and He becomes King *in* each individual, converted heart. One does not negotiate with a king. Jesus is the King of Kings and Lord of Lords and the ultimate Ruler, Comforter and Father in our lives! Christians must learn to trust King Jesus to lead. He knows what's best.

Jeremiah 31:33 - But this shall be the covenant that I will make with the house of Israel; After those days, saith the LORD, **I will put my law in their inward parts, and write it in their hearts;** and will be their God, and they shall be my people.
Hebrews 8:10 - For this is the covenant that I will make with the house of Israel after those days, saith the Lord; **I will put my laws into their mind, and write them in their hearts:** and I will be to

them a God, and they shall be to me a people:

Hebrews 10:16 - This is the covenant that I will make with them after those days, saith the Lord, **I will put my laws into their hearts, and in their minds will I write them;**

Apostles Doctrine

Every member of this generation, that generation, past generations, our generation or some future generation, still had to and still "has" to come through the only "DOOR" (Jesus Christ) to be Kingdom members.

Ephesians 2:20 - And are built upon the foundation of the apostles and prophets, Jesus Christ himself being **the chief cornerstone;**

This encounter, through Gospel belief, includes repentance (a turning from unbelief and a life of sin), baptism in the name of Jesus for the forgiveness of sin and receiving the gift of the Holy Ghost. These steps are the basic foundation stones of the Apostles Doctrine.

Acts 2:38 - Then Peter said unto them, Repent, and be baptized every one of you in the name of Jesus Christ for the remission of sins, and ye shall receive the gift of the Holy Ghost.

Acts 2:42 – **And they continued stedfastly in the apostles doctrine** and fellowship, and in breaking of bread, and in prayers.

Ephesians 2:20 - **And are built upon the foundation of the apostles** and prophets, Jesus Christ himself being the chief corner stone;

Revelation 21:14 - And **the wall of the city had twelve foundations,** and in them the names of the **twelve apostles of the Lamb.**

There is no "back door" or "side door" or "garage door."

John 10:9 - **I am the door:** by me if any man enter in, he shall be saved, and shall go in and out, and find pasture.

John 14:6 - Jesus saith unto him, **I am the way, the truth, and the life: no man cometh unto the Father, but by me.**

1 Timothy 2:5 - For there is one God, and **one mediator between God and men, the man Christ Jesus;**

2 Corinthians 13:5 - Examine yourselves, whether ye be in the faith; prove your own selves. Know ye not your own selves, how that Jesus Christ is in you, except ye be reprobates?

Today's believers have the same opportunity

Most of the first generation believers lost their lives because of their faith in Jesus Christ. It's really no different with today's believers. We all have the same opportunity to have Christ living in us, even if we lose our lives because of our beliefs. What's the difference? Physical death will eventually come to all of us anyway. We are all going to die someday, with or without sticking up for our faith. None of us are going to leave Earth any sooner than our own personal given time. All we have is today. However, we are given the opportunity now to die daily to our old fleshly selves as the Apostle Paul taught and we have the ability to go on to live very productive lives:

1 Corinthians 15:31 - I protest by your rejoicing which I have in Christ Jesus our Lord, I die daily.

The Apostles were not just twelve ordinary men who were called to carry around Jesus' suitcases.

They would go down in history as being called by God for very significant purposes. They are a very important element of God's redemptive plan. They were brought into the complete picture for a reason. The whole "ROCK" foundation of God's New Jerusalem kingdom building rests on their teachings.

No one is special because they belong to this denomination or that denomination, this religion or that religion, or this nationality or that nationality or this political persuasion or that political persuasion. It does not make them anymore right in God's eyes without Christ living in them.

God's Kingdom is too massive to be limited to one certain denomination! The spiritual structure is far too great to give anyone an edge on being, *just us and no more.*

God is not finished with any of today's generation of believers or unbelievers. His followers are all still stuck with each other whether we like it or not and have to live with unbelievers with the hopes of proclaiming and teaching the kingdom of God to them.

God is knocking down divisional walls; just as Jesus Christ predicted would happen and did happen through the Roman armies, to every wall and stone in Old Jerusalem. He is too powerful to be contained to denominational or religious buildings.

The only building God wants to come into is each one of us. It is unfortunate that many Christians throughout church history have missed this very important point.

Stephen reminded the old Jewish rulers that "heaven was God's throne and the earth was His footstool." He was never limited to a temple building.

Acts 7:49 - Heaven is my throne, and earth is my footstool: what house will ye build me? saith the Lord: or what [is] the place of my rest?

Apostle Paul taught that believer's bodies are now the temples of God. His throne is inside of each of us. He rules and reigns from within.

1Corinthians6:19 - What? Know ye not that your body is the temple of the **Holy Ghost which is in you,** which ye have of God, and ye are not your own?

2 Corinthians 13:5 - Examine yourselves, whether ye be in the faith; prove your own selves. Know ye not your own selves, how that **Jesus Christ is in you**, except ye be reprobates?

Galatians 1:16 - **To reveal his Son in me**, that I might preach him among the heathen; immediately I conferred not with flesh and blood:

Galatians 2:20 - I am crucified with Christ: **nevertheless I live; yet not I, but Christ liveth in me:** and the life which I now live in the flesh I live by the faith of the Son of God, who loved me, and gave himself for me.

Galatians 4:6 - And because ye are sons, **God hath sent forth the Spirit of his Son into your hearts,** crying, Abba, Father.

Galatians 6:18 - Brethren, the grace of our **Lord Jesus Christ be with your spirit.** Amen.

The Kingdom of God is like... a Roadmap

What happens when we leave out basic logical understanding in our life's journey?

A man was given an automobile club printed travel roadmap that was supposed to guide him on his drive from Los Angeles, California to Miami, Florida to start a very high paying new job.

It should have been a fairly simple journey for this man. All he had to do was basically follow a straight line on the roadmap for three thousand miles from coast-to-coast with a sharp right turn once he reached the State of Florida. Hundreds of thousands of other drivers have successfully driven this same route before him.

The man's printed roadmap instructed him to drive East on U.S. Route 10 through and out of the State of California, across the entire country on this same highway until he reached the northern border of the State of Florida.

The map then directed the man to make a right turn onto U.S. Route I-95 South and drive that highway straight to the City of Miami.

A problem arose in the man's thinking while driving along his journey. It seems that someone had hand written a note on his map directing him to turn left and drive north when he got to U.S. Route 15.

The man decided after reading the note that it wasn't necessary for him to follow the roadmap's printed directions, thinking the person who wrote the note knew more than the map. So instead, he followed the added handwritten directions and took it upon himself to turn left off of U.S. Route 10 onto U.S. Route 15 and drove North, eventually winding up in all places; Las Vegas, Nevada.

While in Las Vegas the man didn't even get a chance to correct his wrong driving decision. He wasn't in Vegas for more than ten minutes when his car was high jacked with him in it! He was robbed and beaten at gun-point by numerous gang members and left for dead in the desert, until a lost traveler found him laying along the side of a dark deserted road.

The man spent the next eight months in a Las Vegas hospital recovering from his near-death experience.

While in the hospital the man and his family questioned many times on why he didn't just follow the printed map. It was a sure thing! He said over and over that if he would have just followed the roadmap's instructions he would have arrived safely in Miami instead of being in excruciating pain and almost dying three times in a Las Vegas hospital bed.

His life was a total disaster because of his bad decision. Not only did the man lose the high-paying job he was driving to Miami to start, his face was permanently disfigured. And because he had no health insurance, he lost over two hundred thousand dollars in medical expenses.

When studying this tragic situation I totally understand why it is so important to follow a proven plan and to not take matters into my own hands just because I can, or listen to or follow someone who thinks he has a better way.

I've learned over the years that because I was never taught, yet alone followed, clear and simple biblical instructions, my life's journey took many twists and turns with numerous negative consequences.

Looking at the above situation from a biblical perspective I've asked myself why didn't my denomination or even my parents follow God's simple biblical roadmap? It contained instructions, commands and insights that should have been easy to understand, follow and convey.

Instead I was taught another man's way with the biblical roadmap changed with handwritten bad and misguided instructions and commands.

I can understand my parents not knowing better because they were my denomination's victims as well.

Was my denomination so stubborn and self-righteous that it thought it could change God's Word to fit its own misguided roadmap and think by doing so wouldn't have any negative consequences on itself, its followers or their families?

The Apostle Peter was personally given the keys to the kingdom of God from Jesus Christ and he used one of those keys on the Day of Pentecost in 30AD.

The very basis of Christianity began that special Jewish feast day on the fulfillment of Christ's command to His disciples to go out into the world baptizing in the NAME of the father, and of the Son and of the Holy Ghost. (Matthew 28:19)

The Apostle Peter was asked by the people who were gathered around him after he was filled with the Holy Ghost that day on what they should do.

Peter responded to them saying: "Repent, and be baptized every one of you in the name of Jesus Christ for the remission of sins, and you shall receive the gift of the Holy Ghost." (Acts 2:38)

What did these people do after Peter commanded them to be baptized in the name of Jesus Christ?

Did these three thousand souls decide there was a different road they should follow instead of listening to the Apostle Peter and turn away to their own demise?

NO!

Did the three thousand souls question Apostle Peter by asking why he wasn't following Christ's commands in Matthew 28:19? Did they even know about that scripture at that time? Did they even care?

NO!

The three thousand souls clearly followed Peter's commands and were baptized.

"Then they that gladly received his word were baptized: and the same day there were added unto them about three thousand souls." (Acts 2:41)

Could it be that the Apostle Peter was following Jesus' words and using His NAME in baptism?

YES!

Jesus Christ did command to baptize in the NAME of the father, and of the son, and of the Holy Ghost. And that is exactly what the Apostle Peter commanded people should do.

How far has Christianity driven off God's proven road onto its own beaten path just on this one simple doctrine? How far away have we strayed from the Apostle Peter's first commandment to the church back in A.D. 30?

What are Christianity's consequences brought on by itself for not following Jesus Christ's very easy to read and understand roadmap?

I will make this point a bit more personal...

What were my own consequences for my denomination not correctly following and teaching Christ's and Peter's commands?

How far down the wrong road did I have to drive before I realized I was not taught right and was driving in the wrong direction?

How beat up did I have to get?

What darkened road would my body be found on?

My life's journey was a mess for 35 years until I reached the bottom and cried out to God for help on April 28,1981.

I receive a lot of flak when I bring up the subject of baptism, and which is the right or wrong way to perform it.

However, the way it is performed is really not the issue here right now; but studying how far off the road it has gotten us over the years by denominational men taking this matter into their own hands and negating and changing the Apostle Peter's simple roadmap plan of salvation, given to him by Jesus Christ.

Now many divisions are there right now in Christianity caused by not sticking strictly to God's roadmap?

Why are there so many "isms" and denominations based on man-made doctrines, creeds and traditions?

Why aren't the Apostle Peter's words followed and obeyed

correctly? This man was given the keys to the kingdom of God directly from Jesus Christ, Our Lord and Savior, Messiah and King!

I've asked myself many times if it has been worth the cost in my own life after seeing how wrong it was for my denomination not obeying and properly teaching the Word of God.

Denominations willingly moving away from the simple roadmap gospel Jesus Christ and His apostles laid down their lives for has brought on a lot of unnecessary pain and suffering for its members.

My life was tragedy after tragedy for years based on the foundation my religious upbringing instilled in me. I went through hundreds of un-necessary trials and tribulations long before realizing what I was taught was based on outright lies and/or half-truths, if there is any such thing. A lie is a lie. It has nothing to do with being half right and/or half wrong.

When I walk into a prison, jail or drug rehab to minister, I see the damage caused in people's lives by them following their own roadmaps. And those are only the lives I come in contact with each day!

I usually find out later that most of those I've ministered to were either clearly taught wrong doctrine when they were children or taught nothing at all.

Those who have not been taught any biblical truth at all are a lot easier to get through to than those who were taught religious doctrinal lies.

Many of those people don't want to spend any time at all trying to un-due their wrong teachings. They prefer to continue to believe a lie and remain on their own hazardous roads, even though they were warned and instructed they are driving in the wrong direction.

The few of those who do want to change, hungrily accept the Word of God and quickly apply it to their lives. They want to be on and remain on God's simple roadmap as soon as possible.

While in a prison ministry setting I sometimes think about all the lives outside of the prison walls who are in a worst prison in their own misguided beliefs than being locked up in a building. The blessing of serving time prison is at least you know you are in one.

Correctly following Biblical truth really matters a lot to me. It is my roadmap for making it today, tomorrow and forever. It is my responsibility to make sure I stay on the right road and not verve off course one iota.

Looking back on my life now I understand if I had to drive down the wrong road in order to get on the right road because I wasn't given the right roadmap as a child then so be it.

I've had to admit my denomination's mistakes and accept my own responsibilities and consequences for not following God's true roadmap. By being taught wrong doesn't make what I did right. However, as soon as I understood I was on the wrong road, I made sure I corrected my ways as soon as humanly possible to come in line with the Word of God

If the Bible commanded me to be baptized in the NAME of Jesus Christ for the remission of my sins then I did it, even though I was already baptized as a baby and again as a newly born-again Christian in the titles of father, son and Holy Ghost.

"Baptism doesn't matter," a old friend once told me. However, that's a road I refuse to travel. If something is that clear in the Bible as to how Christianity began in A. D. 30 then so be it. I am not going to try to change it nor read something more into it. It's simply is what it is.

I often wonder what other biblical truths my friend thinks don't matter anymore. I get fewer and fewer calls from him nowadays. The last time I heard from him he called me collect from a prison in Utah asking me to send him a Bible. I gathered from his request he was now wanting to use life's real Roadmap.

I prefer to just simply believe and follow God's sure-fire map to success.

By the way... There is not one scripture in the New Testament epistles that reads anyone was ever baptized in the titles 'father, son and holy ghost' or baptized as a baby.

Should I continue on another subject on how mistaken my denomination was on Christ's prophetic words?

Maybe I'll save that one for another day.

Here a question to dwell on until then:

Has misunderstanding and changing God's simple eschatological roadmap for almost two thousand years cause the world any negative consequences?

----

08 JESUS IS A TODAY GOD

Today is the Day of Salvation

Tomorrow never comes… It is always today…

2 Corinthians 6: 2 - For he saith, I have heard thee in a time accepted, and in the day of salvation have I succoured thee: behold, now is the accepted time; behold, **now is the day of salvation.**

The kingdom of God is NOW!!! Enjoy the moment…..

Luke 17:21 - Neither shall they say, Lo here! or, lo there! for, behold, the kingdom of God is within you.

Romans 14:17 - For the kingdom of God is not meat and drink; but righteousness, and peace, and joy in the Holy Ghost.

Jesus is a TODAY God…. here to save and richly bless us now…. today!!! He is the same yesterday, today and forever….. From His virgin birth, death and resurrection to His spiritual coming within on Pentecost 30AD… to His continuous coming within throughout the first century generation (40 years) of believers… to His coming in judgment in AD70 using the Roman armies and to His constant coming within each and every generation up to and including today's… He remains the same… forever!

Jesus Christ the same yesterday, and today, and forever.

Hebrews 13:8 - Jesus Christ the same yesterday, and today, and forever.

We have no fear of tomorrow because tomorrow will take care of itself. Today is the Day of Salvation! Tomorrow will be today… tomorrow.

Matthew 6:34 - Take therefore no thought for the morrow: for the morrow shall take thought for the things of itself. Sufficient unto the day is the evil thereof.

2 Timothy 1:7 - For God hath not given us the spirit of fear; but of power, and of love, and of a sound mind.

Jesus Christ came…. He comes and He continues to come. How many times… one, two, three, four? He comes to whoever will repent and call upon His name. The number of His coming is endless. My guess is as many as there are stars in the heaven and sand on the shore.

Hebrews 11:12 - Therefore sprang there even of one, and him as good as dead, so many as the stars of the sky in multitude, and as the sand which is by the sea shore innumerable.

Our Lord, Savior and King Jesus Christ loves us forever more… and is just as much alive in the world and within believers today as He was during the 1st Century. He came to give us all abundant life throughout the past, present, and future generations.

Luke 1:50 - And his mercy is on them that fear him from generation to generation.

----

09 BECOMING SPIRITUAL

When Nicodemus asked Jesus how a man could be born again in order to see the Kingdom of God (John 3:4), he was not expecting the answer he received.

John 3:4-11 - Nicodemus saith unto him, How can a man be born when he is old? Can he enter the second time into his mother's womb, and be born? Jesus answered, Verily, verily, I say unto thee, Except a man be born of water and of the Spirit, he cannot enter into the kingdom of God. That which is born of the flesh is flesh; and that which is born of the Spirit is spirit. Marvel not that I said unto thee, Ye must be born again. The wind bloweth where it listeth, and thou hearest the sound thereof, but canst not tell whence it cometh, and whither it goeth: so is every one that is born of the Spirit. Nicodemus answered and said unto him, How can these things be? Jesus answered and said unto him, Art thou a master of Israel, and knowest not these things? Verily, verily, I say unto thee, We speak that we do know, and testify that we have seen; and ye receive not our witness.

Nicodemus was taught by Jesus before the Day of Pentecost and we can all learn from this conversation. Nicodemus was a Pharisee and ruler of the Jews. If anyone should have understood what Jesus was teaching, it should have been him. It had to be preached and taught to him so he could properly understand. He and the rest of humanity needed to be taught and exposed to the Gospel. Fortunately for us, we are much better off than Nicodemus because we have the Bible, the written Word of God and the Holy Ghost to guide us into all truth.

Romans 10:14 - How then shall they call on him in whom they have not believed? and how shall they believe in him of whom they have not heard? and how shall they hear without a preacher?

Matthew 4:17 - From that time Jesus began to preach, and to say, Repent: for the kingdom of heaven is at hand.

Matthew 4:23 - And Jesus went about all Galilee, teaching in their synagogues, and preaching the gospel of the kingdom, and healing all manner of sickness and all manner of disease among the people.

Matthew 7:28-29 - And it came to pass, when Jesus had ended these sayings, the people were astonished at his doctrine: For he taught them as one having authority, and not as the scribes.

John 14:26 - But the Comforter, which is the Holy Ghost, whom the Father will send in my name, he shall teach you all things, and bring all things to your remembrance, whatsoever I have said unto you.

Acts 8:35 - Then Philip opened his mouth, and began at the same scripture, and preached unto him Jesus.

Acts 14:7 - And there they preached the gospel.

Acts 20:25 - And now, behold, I know that ye all, among whom I have gone preaching the kingdom of God, shall see my face no more.

Expecting a re-established Kingdom

The first century Jews thought that if God was going to send them their Messiah in their generation He would restore a fleshly physical kingdom that their ancestors experienced. God never approved of that type of Kingdom in the first place so they were mistaken in their present day hopes and beliefs.

Acts 1:6 - When they therefore were come together, they asked of him, saying, Lord, wilt thou at this time restore again the kingdom to Israel?

God's Kingdom was always everlasting. He was always spiritually ruling the world in spite of what fleshly kings (both Israelite and Gentile) thought or did. Therefore, when John the Baptist and Jesus declared the coming Kingdom of God, the Jews and first believers were anticipating escaping their Roman captivity and having a re-established Saul, David or Solomon type king.

The prophet Daniel knew God's kingdom was everlasting. However, humanity never knew there was going to be a way that they could actually have it enter into them. Humanity was and is still is living in God's kingdom, both physically and spiritually.

The mystery the Messiah would bring is that Jesus became the Way for man and God to finally personally fellowship together in God's everlasting Kingdom.

The first century Jews and their leaders didn't fully understand that God Himself would come as Messiah and King to not only Jews but to the Gentiles as well. They should have known better because they had the Holy Scriptures to read and study.

Isaiah 49:6 - And he said, It is a light thing that thou shouldest be my servant to raise up the tribes of Jacob, and to restore the preserved of Israel: I will also give thee for a light to the Gentiles, that thou mayest be my salvation unto the end of the earth.

Daniel 4:3 - How great are his signs! and how mighty are his wonders! his kingdom is an everlasting kingdom, and his dominion is from generation to generation.

Daniel 4:34 - And at the end of the days I Nebuchadnezzar lifted up mine eyes unto heaven, and mine understanding returned unto me, and I blessed the most High, and I praised and honoured him that liveth forever, whose dominion is an everlasting dominion, and his kingdom is from generation to generation:

Daniel 7:14 - And there was given him dominion, and glory, and a kingdom, that all people, nations, and languages, should serve him: his dominion is an everlasting dominion, which shall not pass away, and his kingdom that which shall not be destroyed.

Daniel 7:27 - And the kingdom and dominion, and the greatness of the kingdom under the whole heaven, shall be given to the people of the saints of the most High, whose kingdom is an everlasting kingdom, and all dominions shall serve and obey him.

Psalm 145:13 - Thy kingdom is an everlasting kingdom, and thy dominion endureth throughout all generations.

2 Peter 1:11 - For so an entrance shall be ministered unto you abundantly into the everlasting kingdom of our Lord and Saviour Jesus Christ.

The Everlasting Kingdom of God

The Kingdom of God that Jesus declared and would establish was the opening of the everlasting Kingdom to all of humanity who would place their faith and trust in Him.

Matthew 6:33 – But seek ye first the kingdom of God, and his righteousness; and all these things shall be added unto you.

The coming Messiah was predicted hundreds of years earlier; He had been hoped and prayed for.

Daniel 9:24-27 - Seventy weeks are determined upon thy people and upon thy holy city, to finish the transgression, and to make an end of sins, and to make reconciliation for iniquity, and to bring in everlasting righteousness, and to seal up the vision and prophecy, and to anoint the most Holy. Know therefore and understand, that from the going forth of the commandment to restore and to build Jerusalem unto the Messiah the Prince shall be seven weeks, and threescore and two weeks: the street shall be built again, and the wall, even in troublous times. And after threescore and two weeks shall Messiah be cut off, but not for himself: and the people of the prince that shall come shall destroy the city and the sanctuary; and the end thereof shall be with a flood, and unto the end of the war desolations are determined. And he shall confirm the covenant with many for one week: and in the midst of the week he shall cause the sacrifice and the oblation to cease, and for the overspreading of abominations he shall make it desolate, even until the consummation, and that determined shall be poured upon the desolate.

The Jewish people wanted their Messiah to come, however, when Jesus came and declared He was the Messiah and the spiritual kingdom of God was at hand they were thinking completely opposite of what Jesus taught. They were thinking physical kingdom. Nevertheless, Jesus' spiritual Kingdom message still went forward.

God had a plan and purpose for coming to earth: To save all humanity from sin: Jews first, the Samaritans were second, and then came the Gentiles. Jesus became the Door all would have to open and go through in order to have His everlasting spiritual Kingdom enter into them.

Mark 1:15 - And saying, The time is fulfilled, and the kingdom of God is at hand: repent ye, and believe the gospel.

Luke 17:21 - Neither shall they say, Lo here! or, lo there! for, behold, the kingdom of God is within you.

John 18:36 - Jesus answered, My kingdom is not of this world: if my kingdom were of this world, then would my servants fight, that I should not be delivered to the Jews: but now is my kingdom not from hence.

Romans 1:16 - For I am not ashamed of the gospel of Christ: for it is the power of God unto salvation to everyone that believeth; to the Jew first, and also to the Greek.

Romans 14:17 - For the kingdom of God is not meat and drink; but righteousness, and peace, and joy in the Holy Ghost.

Spirit Falls, Enters, Rests and Comes Upon

The Jewish religious and political leaders of that generation didn't seem the least bit concerned with you or me finding salvation or access to the everlasting Kingdom of God. Did they even care about their own eternal security let alone ours? They behaved selfishly and did not properly understand what was expected of their Messiah.

However, Abraham knew all about it. He and many others walked the faith walk but he didn't experience the spiritual fullness of God as we have today. Abraham only looked. He did know that through his Seed came the Door into the Kingdom of God and entrance into the New Jerusalem, the heavenly city.

Hebrews 11:10 - For he (Abraham) looked for a city which hath foundations, whose builder and maker is God.

Galatians 3:16 - Now to Abraham and his seed were the promises made. He saith not, And to seeds, as of many; but as of one, And to thy seed, which is Christ.

Acts 3:25 - Ye are the children of the prophets, and of the covenant which God made with our fathers, saying unto Abraham, And in thy seed shall all the kindreds of the earth be blessed.

Hebrews 11:16 - But now they desire a better country, that is, an heavenly: wherefore God is not ashamed to be called their God: for he hath prepared for them a city.

John 10:7 - Then said Jesus unto them again, Verily, verily, I say unto you, I am the door of the sheep.

John 10:9 - I am the door: by me if any man enter in, he shall be saved, and shall go in and out, and find pasture.

The Spirit of the Lord fell, came, rested upon and only entered certain prophets, priests or kings in the Old Testament. He never came "into" people like He did on the Day of Pentecost.

Ezekiel 11:5 - And the Spirit of the LORD fell upon me, and said unto me, Speak; Thus saith the LORD; Thus have ye said, O house of Israel: for I know the things that come into your mind, every one of them.

Numbers 11:25 - And the LORD came down in a cloud, and spake unto him, and took of the spirit that was upon him, and gave it unto the seventy elders: and it came to pass, that, when the spirit rested upon them, they prophesied, and did not cease.

Ezekiel 2:2 - And the spirit entered into me when he spake unto me, and set me upon my feet, that I heard him that spake unto me.

Judges 3:10 - And the Spirit of the LORD came upon him, and he judged Israel, and went out to war: and the LORD delivered Chushanrishathaim king of Mesopotamia into his hand; and his hand prevailed against Chushanrishathaim.

John the Baptist is the only human mentioned in the Bible who was actually born filled with the Holy Ghost even from his mother's womb.

Luke 1:15 - For he (John the Baptist) shall be great in the sight of the Lord, and shall drink neither wine nor strong drink; and he (John the Baptist) shall be filled with the Holy Ghost, even from his mother's womb.

----

10 CHRISTIAN BASED TREATMENT PROGRAMS

Listed below are Christian-based programs offering help. For other types of treatment modalities please search the Internet or check your local telephone directory.

ADULT PROGRAMS
For more info please see: martyangelo.com/substance_abuse1.htm

Agape Home - Christian-based safe resting place for Jesus Christ to restore women with or without children to wholeness in a loving family atmosphere. Located in Moore Haven, Florida.

Alcoholics for Christ® - Christian-based inter-denominational, non-profit, fellowship that ministers to Alcoholics or Substance abusers, Family members, and Adult Children. Nationwide.

Alcoholics Victorious - network of Christian-based support groups offering a safe environment where recovering people gather together and share their experience, strength, and hope. Nationwide.

Broken Shackle Ranch - Christian-based residential school for abandoned, abused, and underprivileged young men ages 16 to 20 years old. Located in central Georgia.

Calvary Ranch - Christian-based program that treats chemical dependency and addictions of many kinds in a rural Christian setting. Located in Lakeside, California.

Camp Hebron - Christian-based long-term, residential recovery program. Located in Indianapolis, Indiana.

Canaan Land Ministries - Christian-based program. Located in Autaugaville, AL.

ChooseHelp - offers a range of inpatient alcohol and drug rehab programs including Christian-based counseling. St Pete Beach, Florida and Laguna Beach, California.

Celebrate A New Life - Christian-based Residential Drug Rehab and Alcohol Treatment Program, located in the coastal communities of Orange County Southern California.

Celebrate Recovery - Christian-based program providing fellowship and celebration of God's healing power in lives through eight recovery principles. Nationwide.

Christians in Recovery® - Christian-based program dedicated to recovering Christians to mutual sharing of faith, strength, and hope. Nationwide.

Christian Recovery Resource Centers - information about Christian and Christian-track treatment programs, Christian sober living, Christian Counseling, and Christian recovery fellowships. Worldwide.

Christian Recovery International - Christian-based coalition of ministries dedicated to helping the Christian community. Nationwide.

Christian Recovery Resources Database - Christian-based search world-wide listing of support groups, residential programs, organizations, counselors and more. Nationwide.

Dream Center - non-profit Christian-based outreach dedicated to helping inner cities. Located in Los Angeles, California.

Dunklin Memorial Camp - Christian-based program for the spiritual, emotional, and physical a regeneration of alcoholics and drug addicts. Okeechobee, Florida.

Eastham Home for Women - faith-based, long-term, residential recovery program for women who struggle with addiction issues. Located in Boynton Beach, Florida

Eternal Awakenings - Christian-based drug rehab center that provides a beautiful, serene atmosphere conducive to spiritual reflection and Christian recovery. Located in Gonzales, Texas

Faith Farm Ministries - faith-based, long-term, residential recovery program for men and women who struggle with addiction issues, with three campuses in Ft. Lauderdale, Boynton Beach, and Okeechobee, Florida.

Foundry Rescue Mission and Recovery Center - offers a comprehensive array of Christian services that provide preventive solutions for low-income individuals and families in the community. Located in Bessemer, Alabama.

Fresh Start Ministries - year-long, Christian-based residential substance abuse program for men. Located in Orlando, Florida.

Full Circle Outreach Ranch - Christian-based residential live-in community facility. Located in the City of Norco – Riverside, California.

Global World Challenge - Christian-based network of over 250 Teen Challenge centers in more than 80 countries. Worldwide.

Good Samaritan's Inn - offers effective, Christian-based counseling and recovery in the form of a 6-month residential program for men 18 years and older. Hamilton, Ohio.

Home of Grace - offers a strong Christian-based program to meet the needs of those struggling in addiction. The women's home is located in Gautier, Mississippi. The men's home is located in Vancleave, Mississippi.

International Christian Recovery Coalition - informal, international fellowship comprised of Christian leaders and workers in the recovery arena. Tucson, AZ.

Isaiah House - Christian-based program helping men with life controlling issues such as drug and alcohol addictions. Located in Hustonville, Kentucky.

JC's Recovery Center - Christian-based program that assists people recover from alcohol and drug addiction using the 12 Steps of Recovery and the Bible. Hollywood, Florida

John 3:16 Ministries - Christian-based boot camp for men with addictions. Located in Charlotte, AR.

Liberty Lodge - Christian-based providing a man with a structured home environment where he can begin to help himself achieve goals of sobriety and health. Located in Titusville, Florida.

Lighthouse with Healthcare Solutions - Christian-based "single-point contact" that provides no cost, confidential assistance to those struggling with drug and alcohol addictions, eating disorders, mood, anxiety and stress disorders, sexual addictions, gambling and other life-controlling behaviors. Located in Newtown, PA.

NET Training Institute - provides Christian-based training in counseling, addiction, prevention, and recovery support ministry. Located in Orlando, Florida.

New Life Home for Women and Children - Christian-based, long-term, residential drug and alcohol crisis intervention facility for women and their children. Located in Manchester, New Hampshire.

No Longer Bound - Christian-based drug and alcohol program for adult males ages 18 and up. Located in Cumming, Georgia.

Our Father's House - Christian-based residential program helping people kick addictions. Located in Saco, Maine.

Overcomers Outreach - unique Christian-based ministry of more than 1,000 support groups. Nationwide.

Refuge Ranch - Christian-based residential drug regeneration ministry for adult women. Located in Okeechobee, Florida.

Renewal Christian Treatment and Recovery - Brookhaven Hospital drug rehabilitation program incorporating Christian-based 12-Steps Towards Recovery. Located in Tulsa, OK.

Set Free - network of Christian-based evangelical churches and rehab centers. Nationwide.

St. Anthony Foundation - Christian-based program that provides food, shelter, clothing of those in need. Located in San Francisco, California.

Teen Challenge for Women - Christian-based program for healing, joy and restoration for women who are 18 and older. Davie, Florida.

Teen Challenge USA - Christian-based substance abuse program. Nationwide.

Teen Challenge of Southern California - provides youth, adults, women and children an effective and comprehensive Christian-based solution to drug and alcohol addiction. Located in Southern California.

The Women's Refuge - Christian-based program for women who are experiencing emotional, mental and spiritual problems. Vero Beach, Florida.

Transformations Treatment Center - Christian-based 30 to 90 day drug and alcohol treatment program that offers luxury apartments with private rooms during treatment. Located in Delray Beach, Florida.

Transitional Living Program - Christian-based 12-month program established to provide the ex-offender with a safe residence. Located in Tampa, Florida.

U-Turn for Christ - Christian-based Discipleship Ranch Facility involved in volunteer work throughout the community. Located in Perris, California.

Victory Outreach - Christian-based Pentecostal denomination with some 150,000 members and adherents, many of whom suffered from substance abuse. Hundreds of locations worldwide.

Walter Hoving Home - non-profit, Christian-based rehabilitation center serving women 18 years. Three locations: Las Vegas, New York, California.

Wheeler's Hebron Center - long-term, Christian-based residential drug and alcohol treatment recovery. Located in Bloomington, Indiana.

YOUTH PROGRAMS
For more info please see: martyangelo.com/substance_abuse1.htm

Abundant Life Academy - Christian boarding schools designed exclusively for unmotivated gifted troubled teens. Located in Jesup, Georgia.

Broken Shackle Ranch - Christian youth home that specializes in helping young men ages 16-19 by teaching them responsibility, discipline, work ethic, and moral values. Located in Davisboro, Georgia.

Gethsemane Ranch - provides a place for the encouragement of today's youth, to establish solid values and beliefs, and to become settled firmly in Christian character. Located in Okeechobee, FL.

His Mansion Ministries - community of Christians using Biblical counsel to help dysfunctional young adults. Located in Hillsboro, New Hampshire.

Idaho Youth Ranch - provides residential treatment, group homes, adoption and other services for troubled, disturbed, delinquent or abused children and adolescents. Located in Boise, Idaho.

Juveniles for Jesus - Christian-based, volunteer-driven, and connected with church and community for incarcerated youth. Located in Clearwater, Florida.

Living Free Recovery Services - Christian treatment program that is licensed by the Minnesota Department of Human Services to serve individuals 13 years of age and older. Located in Brooklyn Park, Minnesota.

Mission Teens, Inc. - Christian treatment program for the desperate. Various locations. Based in Norma, New Jersey.

Paul Anderson Youth Home - residential home that provides Christian rehabilitation for young men between the ages of 16 and 21 who are seeking an alternative to incarceration. Located in Vidalia, Georgia.

Real Life Children's Ranch - provides a safe, nurturing, family style environment for children. Located in Okeechobee, Florida.

Straight Ahead Ministries - a juvenile justice resource center. Main office is located in Worcester, Massachusetts.

----

11 ABOUT THE AUTHOR

Marty Angelo worked in the entertainment business from 1965 to 1980 as a television producer, record promoter, disk jockey, restaurant/nightclub owner and personal manager for rock 'n' roll bands. He received his first professional breaks from the late guitar legend Jimi Hendrix and Beatle George Harrison.

Though at times Angelo thought he achieved success, internally he always felt emptiness in his heart. He sensed his life had neither real meaning nor true purpose. Nothing ever seemed to matter to him. Therefore, he lived an out-of-control sin-riddled lifestyle.

Angelo was arrested in 1980 for two counts of possession of cocaine. Through this life-shattering event he experienced a "new beginning," a dramatic and electrifying conversion to Christianity. This miracle happened in 1981 prior to serving two-and-a-half years in a federal prison. God forgave Marty's sins, blessed him with eternal life and filled the void in Marty's heart with His Holy Spirit. His life finally began to matter and it took on a new meaning as he discovered God's true plan and purpose.

Marty Angelo helped many prisoners during his incarceration explaining to them that if God can change his life He can change anybody... including hardened convicts, drunkards and drug addicts. Many followed his advice. Marty also graduated from four colleges while incarcerated, receiving ministerial degrees and licenses to minister from two major denominations.

Angelo was released from prison in 1984 and is living his life as an example to other ex-convicts and former drug-addicts and alcoholics who want to serve God and be used by Him for His glory.

For more than 30 years, Angelo has worked with various ministries such as; The Fort Lauderdale Rescue Tabernacle (Faith Farm), Teen Challenge of Southern California, Chuck Colson's Prison Fellowship Ministries and The Drug Abuse Foundation of Palm Beach County.

Marty Angelo is currently a full-time minister to prisoners, substance abusers and troubled celebrities. His nationwide ministry reaches out to prisons & jails, rehabs & support groups, schools & churches and various celebrities.

Celebrity Outreach

Marty Angelo's 15 years in the entertainment industry has given him a special burden for today's celebrities who are doing the same drugging, drinking and law breaking he did while living in the fast lane in the music business.

No one warned Marty of the consequences of leading such a life nor offered him any alternative direction. He prays others will learn by his mistakes and seek a better life.

Marty believes as a Christian he has an obligation to encourage troubled celebrities and others to try a better road to travel; one that leads to everlasting peace, happiness and a new life that truly does matter. Angelo donates his services to celebrities using letters, books, faith-based rehab referrals and court appearances.

Marty Angelo is the Author of Nine Books

Once Life Matters: A New Beginning! - 1st Edition
(ISBN: 9780961895440)

Vision of New Jerusalem: Now!
(ISBN: 9780615562438)

Once Life Matters: A New Beginning! - 2nd Edition
(ISBN: 9780985107727)

Inspirational Insights: Christ in You!
(ISBN: 9780985107734)

Lives that Matter: Letters from Prison
(ISBN: 9780985107741)

Addiction is NOT a Disease
(ISBN: 9780985107772)

Names, Titles and Manifestations of God
(ISBN: 9780985107758)

Truth Be Told
(ISBN: 9780985107789)

Celebrity Outreach
(ISBN: 9780985107796)

YouTube Videos: Speeches, Church Services, Talks

https://www.youtube.com/playlist?list=PLaP1J3pUWaH5YROHE
b9orKoDiG9NLC74J

Radio and Television Interviews

https://www.youtube.com/playlist?list=PLaP1J3pUWaH7OeB7w
H_XOl3wnp1_q_Bvj

Amazon.com Author's Book Page

http://www.amazon.com/Marty-Angelo/e/B002MN1660

Media Appearances

Mr. Angelo has made numerous television and radio appearances:

Television

AOL Television, Canada's "100 Huntley Street", CBN's "The 700 Club", CBS - "Sunday Morning", CNN's TruTv - "In Session", Daystar's "Celebration", Gospel Tube, I'm Just Sayin' Show, Larry King, Life Story, MTV, Prison Outreach Radio and TV Show, Storyology, Trinity Broadcasting's "Praise the Lord", VH1, YouTube.

Radio

Adrienna Turner Radio Show, Alive in Christ Radio Show, Bob Dutko Radio Show, Crossroad Connection Radio Show, David Allen Radio Show, Desi Radio, Drew Marshall Radio Show, Frank Murphy - FM in the AM, Frank Pastore Radio Show, Gianni Hayes Radio Show, Hairy Tics Variety Radio Show, Inside Scoop Radio Show, Intentional Living, Itunes Podcast, Jesse Peterson Radio Show, Joey Reynolds Radio Show, Lifeline with Kurt Goff,

Morning Live Powerfully, Radio Show with Jon and Rhonda, Neil Boron Radio Show, Not Just Talkin' the Talk Radio Show, Once Life Matters Radio Show, Prison Outreach Radio and TV Show, The Journey Radio Show, United News & Information Radio Show, "Unshackled" - a radio show dramatization of Marty Angelo's testimony, Vital Connection, Wiley Drake Radio Show

In addition, Angelo has been quoted in various newspapers, magazines and internet websites and blogs, including:

Newspapers, Magazines, Websites, Blogs

ABC News, Access Hollywood, Alipes News, All Things Deep, Ask the Experts, Associated Press, Austin American-Statesman, Authors Den, Baltimore Business Journal, Beaumont Enterprise, Bible Glory, Biblical News and Review, Book Publishing Industry Today, Boston Globe, Brooklyn News, Buffalo News, Business First of Columbus, Business Journal of Greater Milwaukee, Business Journal of the Greater Triad Area, California Drug Rehab, Christian Headlines, Christian Life News, Christian News Tweets, Christian Signal, Cincinnati Business Courier, Contact Music, Connecticut Post, Denver Business Journal, Denver Post, Edinburgh Days Out, Entertainers Resource Directory, Entertainment Today, Everyday Christian Living, Examiner, Ezerin'Com Communication Agency, Faithful News, Faith News Network, God Rev, Good News Daily, Google News, Help Drug Addicts, Hire Life Science, Holly Scoop, Hollywood Today, Huffington Post, India Infoline, Inside Journal, Inside Scoop, IT Industry Today, Jailhouse Journal Magazine, Jossip, Kansas Free Press, KGO-TV ABC-7 (San Francisco CA), KTAL-TV Channel 6 Shreveport, Las Vegas Business Press, Los Angeles Daily News, Los Angeles Times, Manchester Matters, Media-online.ru, Mega News Network: Entertainment, Mercury News, Methadone Recovery, Ministry Watch, Minneapolis / St. Paul Business Journal, MSN News, myMotherLode.com, NBC News, New Mexico Business Weekly, New York Times, News Info Guide,

News Time, Newsblaze, News Week Daily, North Bay Christian News, Ok Magazine, One News Now, Opinions, Pacific Business News, Palm Beach Post, Perez Hilton, Pasadena Star News, Pittsburgh Business Times, Press-Enterprise, Prison Living Magazine, Radar Online, Pulse Entertainment, Readers View, Red Orbit, Recovery Helper, Rehab America, Religion Today, Religious Resources, Reuters, Rolling Stone Magazine, Sacramento Bee, San Antonio Business Journal, San Antonio News, San Diego News, San Jose Business Journal, Santa Cruz Sentinel, Seattle Post Intelligencer, Seattle Times Society and Lifestyle, SF Gate, Stamford Advocate, Star Pulse, Star Tribune, Student Operated Press (The SOP), Teen Options, Telegram, The Prison Insider, TMZ, Treatments for Addictions, Trends Buzz, Triangle Business Journal, US Magazine, Village Voice, Washington Times, Wichita Business Journal, Wichita Christian News, World Christian Newsroom

----

www.ingramcontent.com/pod-product-compliance
Lightning Source LLC
Chambersburg PA
CBHW071617040426
42452CB00009B/1368